The Party Dress

First published in the UK by Scriptum Editions
63 Edith Grove, London, SW10 0LB

Created by Bound Creative
Copyright © 2007 Co & Bear Productions (UK) Ltd
Photographs copyright © various (see credits)
Text copyright © Co&Bear Productions (UK) Ltd
Co & Bear Productions (UK) Ltd identify Alexandra Black
as author of the work.

Art Director: Bradd Nicholls
Art and Production Consultant: Lisa Anne

Publishers: Beatrice Vincenzini & Francesco Venturi
Executive Director: David Shannon

First edition
ISBN 978 1 902686 59 2
10 9 8 7 6 5 4 3 2 1
Repro by Bright Arts Pty
Printed in Italy by DeaPrinting

The Party Dress

ALEXANDRA BLACK

SCRIPTUM EDITIONS

Contents

"Drink, and dance and laugh and lie/Love the reeling midnight through/
For tomorrow we shall die!/(But, alas, we never do.)"
Dorothy Parker

Introduction

"How absurd that any sane man should suppose/That a lady would go to a ball in the clothes/No matter how fine, that she wears every day!"

William Allen Butler, Nothing to Wear

The legendary editor of American *Vogue*, Diana Vreeland, adored dressing up. In her autobiography, written in 1984 at the age of eighty-one, she vividly recalls the night of her coming out party in 1923. "My dress was white, naturally," she wrote. "It was copied from Poiret – white satin with a fringed skirt to give it *un peu de mouvement* and a pearl and diamond stomacher to hold the fringe back before it sprang." With it she wore velvet slippers "that were lacquer red" and carried red camellias, of which her mother strongly disapproved as they were traditionally carried by the demimondaines of the nineteenth century when they had their periods, to indicate they were not "available" to their gentleman.

"I carried the camellias anyway," writes Vreeland. "They were so beautiful I had to assume that no else at the party knew what my mother knew."

While not all of us can recall our formative fashions in such passionate detail, many can remember at least something about their first childhood party dress. For some it will have been love at first sight, with a pretty confection of hailspot voile, or pink tulle, or stiff taffeta. For others it will have been a source of frustration and embarassment, making its wearer feel painfully self-conscious. By adulthood, though, most women have realised with delight the pleasure and power inherent in that special occasion dress.

Cecil Beaton's fashion photograph from the 1950s (opposite), captures the transforming power of a truly beautiful dress. The gown, embroidered with sprigs of dainty flowers and tied with an enormous lavender silk bow, is soft and feminine but has great physical presence. Likewise, the magnificent Charles James-designed ball gowns in dusky pastel shades (previous pages), appear romantic, yet their sculptural qualities and the swathes of fabric used in the skirts help give the models wearing them a powerful poise.

Chapter One

The Masquerade

"More than one woman since Lot's wife has betrayed herself by looking back, but I can't help shedding a nostalgic tear for the decline of my favourite entertainment — the costume party."

Elsa Maxwell

O f all parties, the masquerade is without doubt the most thrilling. The masquerade is one of the oldest forms of exclusive social entertainment, and one with an especially exciting, and subversive, undercurrent. For where other types of parties require that you come as a more exaggerated version of yourself — more beautiful at a ball, more comely at a cocktail party, more romantic at a garden party and more refined at a wedding party — the masquerade allows you to experiment with a completely different identity.

Hidden behind a mask, the wearer has the freedom to forget everyday norms and niceties, and the power to take on a new persona. It is as if the rules that govern normal life and conduct are dispensed with for one night only. No wonder that the masquerade has become such an evocative, and sometimes potent, event.

For many historians and cultural commentators, the idea of the costume ball, or masquerade, is equated with sexual freedom and certain union. In putting on a disguise, or at least appearing to take on a new persona, the party-goer takes a step into the unknown. The act of concealment creates a sense of fascination, sometimes bordering on fetishistic. When a person surrenders their own identity there is

Throughout the ages the masquerade, or masque, has been a favourite entertainment of royalty. In the seventeenth and eighteenth centuries, the French court at Versailles was particularly fond of costume parties, and lavish events were held at the palace several times a week. Given the strict formality of court life, the donning of a disguise gave the wearer the chance to escape from the pressures of duty and position.

a danger also that their sense of moral responsibility is also forfeited. In earlier centuries the act of attending a masquerade complicitly signalled a readiness to sexual intimacy with a stranger, or if not a stranger at least a person whose identity might be concealed, even if easily guessed.

The word masquerade is built on the stem, masque, meaning mask. According to Terry Castle, in *Masquerades and Civilisation*, the word masquerade came into the English language to describe particular festivals held in continental Europe. Castle writes that "the early forms mascardo and mascurado appear in English in the late sixteenth and seventeenth century, but only in the context of foreign custom. In his *Introduction to Practicall Musicke* of 1597, Thomas Morley speaks of the Italian 'mascaradoes' and in a 1660 translation of Vincent Le Blanc's *Travels*, Francis Brooke mentions the Spaniards' 'Mascuradoes' at which they disguised themselves as devils."

The modern idea of the masquerade ball is thought to have evolved from the masque, a type of entertainment in the courts of Italy for which the courtiers, and even kings and queens, became performers, donning masks or painting their faces to take on a dramatic or dancing role.

To best tell the story of the masquerade we need to return to fourteenth century France, where during the reign of King Charles VI, the passion for costume balls reached fever pitch. Here was the scene of one of the first court balls ever recorded. It was also one of the most decadent, and destructive.

The notorious *bal des sauvages*, or wild men's ball, was held on January 28, 1393, by King Charles VI of France and his wife Isabeau of Bavaria, Queen of France. Under the court of the Valois, late-fourteenth century Paris was a cosmopolitan city, and high society enjoyed all kinds of parties and pleasures. However, the *bal des sauvages* was to be so excessive that not even the most seasoned Parisian party-goer could fail to be impressed. The occasion was the wedding of one of the Queen's ladies-in-waiting.

It is not clear whether the masquerade ball was dreamed up by the King, who suffered from bouts of mental illness, or the Queen, who was known throughout Europe for her fashionable ways and frivolous habits. In any case, the ball was set for the Tuesday before Candlemas, 1393, and everyone invited expected it to be an uproarious occasion. The bride-to-be was a widow and it was customary at court to celebrate with complete abandon at the nuptial celebrations of a widow.

The setting was the King's own lavish residence, the Hotel de Saint-Pol, a vast complex of buildings connected by galleries, in the east of Paris. There were

Anne, Countess of Rossse was a passionate lover of fancy dress, and from a young age played dress-ups with her brother Oliver Messel, who reigned as Britain's leading costume designer from the 1930s to the 1960s. Anne was a society beauty and attended all the great fancy dress balls of the 1920s and 1930s, often wearing her brother's creations.

costume historian Harold Acton's descriptions of the costumes it is hard to imagine a royal household quite so fantastically and daringly attired:

> The ladies wore stupendous head-dresses shaped like the horns of buffalo and unicorn, so that they had to bend double to pass through doorways, and they dragged long trains after them in which it was easy to trip up. Their bosoms were almost bare, but their sleeves floated to the ground. Most of them dwarfed the men, whose doublets were embroidered with everything under the sun: astronomy, botany, natural history had inspired the most original designs, and some wore zigzag musical notes in front and behind, or Gothic riddles of questionable morality. As the ladies wore horns on their heads, the men wore horns on their toes for their shoes curved upwards. Those who tired of dancing played trinquet, quartes or chess, or went out to tease the tigers in the menagerie and listen to the twitterings of tropical birds.

also magnificent landscaped grounds comprising courtyards, a number of formal gardens, a cherry orchard, a menagerie housing wild animals, aviaries and an aquarium.

Guests had been dancing for the best part of the day after the wedding ceremony, before the masquerade ball really got under way in the evening hours. Revellers paused to sit down for an enormous supper of some thirty courses, featuring every kind of meat and game imaginable accompanied by matching sauces, pickles and truffle creams, and then the party moved on to the ballroom. Reading

However, it was the King who reserved for himself and his companions the honour of being most outrageously attired. Charles and five of his friends

The popularity of the masquerade has endured for centuries, from the elaborate masques of the Court of King James I of England in the sixteenth century (above left) to the famous Beistegui Ball (opposite) held in September 1951 by Don Carlos de Beistegui, heir to a Mexican silver fortune, at his Venetian palazzo.

had hatched a plan to disguise themselves as wild satyrs of the woods. The idea was that at the height of the ball, the six would change into their secret costumes and surprise the assembled guests.

So it was that just before midnight the King and his companions gathered in private and were stitched into their hairy costumes, made from linen and covered with resin to which flax had been attached to give the impression of human hair. The ballroom candles were dimmed in readiness, the music stopped, and to the sound of drum beats, the six satyrs burst into the room, leaping and whirling amidst the startled guests, chasing the ladies, embracing and nuzzling their favourites.

According to Acton, the story goes that the King's younger brother the Duc d'Orleans who had been in another hall all the while, entered the main ballroom, and was startled to see the six wild men frolicking, most particularly with his mistress. He moved closer with his torch bearer to see what was happening and in that instant a spark flew from the torch and set the nearest satyr ablaze. The flames jumped from one satyr to the next, fuelled by the resin that covered the linen costumes. One of the "wild men" saved himself by plunging into the water butt in the adjoining butlery, where the plates and cups were rinsed, although he was disfigured by the fire. Four others died in the flames. But what of the King, whose identity no one had guessed? He had been engaged in a playful tussle with the Duchess of Berri when the sparks began to fly, so was spared the fate of his noblemen. Yet the dramatic events seem to have unhinged the King, suffering as he already did from mental illness.

As Acton explains, after the ball the King seemed to thoroughly reject his real identity and responsibilities. "He no longer wished to be himself, either Charles or King," writes Laver. "He denied that he was married or had a child. Perhaps this was not madness … do not we all have moments when we would like to be somebody else, and is this not one of the reasons why fancy dress balls remain so popular."

Indeed, that fateful ball, which in later years became known as "Le Bal des Ardents" or "The Ball of the Burning Men" did nothing to diminish the appeal of the masquerade, or costume ball. No doubt the event cooled the ardour of the royal couple for such diversions, but it was not long before their successors embraced this most intriguing of parties.

Catherine de Medici is typically credited for setting the vogue for masked balls, indeed raising the bar for all kinds of parties, from wedding celebrations to dinner parties to grand balls and masquerades. Born in Florence to the wealthy Medici family, she married into the French royal family, becoming

The Duke and Duchess of York, later King George V and Queen Mary, in costume as the 3rd Earl of Cumberland and a lady at the court of Marguerite de Valois for a fancy dress ball held at Devonshire House in London in 1897. Half a century later, Hollywood royalty in the form of Orson Welles donned historical garb at the Beistegui Ball of 1951 (overleaf, left), while Zac Posen's contemporary costume (overleaf, right) is fit for a twenty-first-century princess.

Posen
for
K.K

the bride of Henri, Duc d'Orleans, soon to be King Henri II. As Queen of France between 1547 and 1559, Catherine de Medici became renowned for her love of intrigue, and, fittingly, she loved the thrill of the masquerade ball. In political terms she was considered powerful and ruthless. Culturally, she was incredibly influential, elevating the French court to even greater heights of elegance. She introduced the practice of wearing scented gloves, is said to have worn the first high-heeled shoes, and also to have invented lip gloss, mixing beeswax with red pigment. Among other niceties she brought with her from Italy ballet, Italian cuisine — including sorbet, macaroons, veal and truffles — the habit of eating with a fork and the art of good table manners.

There is no doubt that as a Medici she was raised in great style and on her arrival in France it was clear that she already possessed rather extravagant tastes. She was a natural hostess and prided herself on her reputation for throwing a great party. There may have been other motivations, too. As an Italian in a French court, and with her place as Queen jeopardised by her husband's beautiful mistress Diane de Poitiers, Catherine needed every wile and wit to keep herself, and her children, in a position of power. Henri was so smitten with Diane that he gave her not only the crown jewels but also the gift of the Chateau de Chenonceau. Catherine had reason to be worried, and used her entertaining prowess to impress the court and improve her stature.

The masquerade ball in particular proved an ideal setting for political machinations and personal manipulations. She would have been very familiar with the Italian Renaissance tradition of costume balls. They were especially popular in Venice, where masquerading became something of an obsession as early as the thirteenth century.

The Venice Carnival, was first mentioned in written records in 1268. The carnival was meant to celebrate the end of Lent and, in the style of pagan Roman festivals sanctioned licentiousness and abandon in a deliberate overturning of social conventions. In fact Venetian lawmakers were kept busy for a few hundred years regulating the wearing of masks and attempting to restrict the behaviour of revellers. A decree made in January 1458 banned men in womens' costume from entering convents (to prevent them pestering the nuns and in some cases assaulting them). Another decree in 1608 spelt out that masks could only be worn during the days of the carnival and at official banquets, but at no other time. While in 1776 a new law meant that every woman going to the theatre must wear a mask and cloak. The mask makers themselves had their own laws and guild, and enjoyed an elevated position in Venetian society.

The Venetian-style carnival balls had evolved into something rather more refined and self-conscious in the Florentine court, as Catherine de Medici would have known them. These masquerades, or

❦ Originality is key to a successful party outfit: Singer sewing machine heiress Daisy Fellowes at the Beistegui Ball of 1951 (opposite); A pregnant Marisa Berenson at the Rothschild's Proust Ball of 1971 (overleaf, left); and the eccentric socialite Marchesa Casati in 1890 wearing a diamond-encrusted costume designed by couturier Charles Worth to represent "Light" (overleaf, right).

masques, were essentially elaborate dances in which participants attended in costume and mask, often representing characters from mythology, religion or literature. Catherine was a keen dancer and once installed in Paris went to great lengths to give her courtiers dancing lessons, using ballet instructors brought from Florence, specifically so that they could participate in dramatic masques.

On Henri's death she reclaimed the chateau and extensively remodelled it to provide a suitable venue for her parties. She redesigned the gardens to eradicate any sign of Diane's taste, and built a new wing of which the centrepiece was a huge ballroom. It was beautifully decorated with a floor of Italian tiles to make it well suited to dancing. Most spectacularly of all, it was constructed to be partially suspended over the river that flowed through the chateau grounds, and was the scene of many spectacular masked balls.

Of all the French queens, few could rival Marie Antoinette for the frequency and elaborateness of her masquerades. A lover of fashion, somewhat bored, and no doubt influenced by the stylistically intense and sophisticated environment of the court at Versailles, Marie Antoinette excelled at entertainments of the masked kind.

Historian Caroline Weber hints that Marie Antoinette may have been influenced by her grandfather-in-law, Louis XIV, the Sun King, a keen lover of masques. In any event, the young Queen decided to host two parties a week, one of which would be a masquerade ball. "For the first of these events," writes Weber in

Queen of Fashion: What Marie Antoinette Wore to the Revolution, "held on January 9, 1775, Marie Antoinette drew her inspiration from a recent snowfall, selecting 'Norwegians and Lapps' as the theme. Outfitted in sumptuous, faux-Scandinavian attire provided at the Queen's behest by the Superintendant des Menus Plaisir (Steward of Small Pleasures), Papillon de La Ferté, and his staff, courtiers flocked to the party and lingered well past dawn."

Perhaps because of her precarious political position, Marie Antoinette focused herself on repeating the success of her masked ball, each week settling on a new theme to capture the attention of the Versailles courtiers. Caroline Weber notes that "Sometimes Marie Antoinette prescribed an alluringly simple scheme for the colours and fabrics her guests were to wear: for example 'white taffeta with flowing tulle' for the ladies, and 'blue velvet with white, [blue-embroidered] waistcoats' for the men. On other occasions, she drew on her knowledge of French royal history to re-create the Renaissance courts of Francois I and Henri IV. For these gatherings party-goers were instructed to wear stylised sixteenth-century costume: trunk hose and jerkins for the gentlemen, gabled hoods and bell-shaped farthingale skirts for their damsels, and starched white ruffs for every neck." At one such Renaissance Ball, Marie Antoinette attended as Gabrielle d'Estrées, the

The exuberance of carnivale is captured here in a peacock blue Chanel ensemble, with a shimmering, armour-like bodice, fluid satin skirt and exotic accessories, photographed by Arthur Elgort. Coco Chanel understood the transforming power of evening clothes: "Be a caterpillar by day and a butterfly by night," she once said.

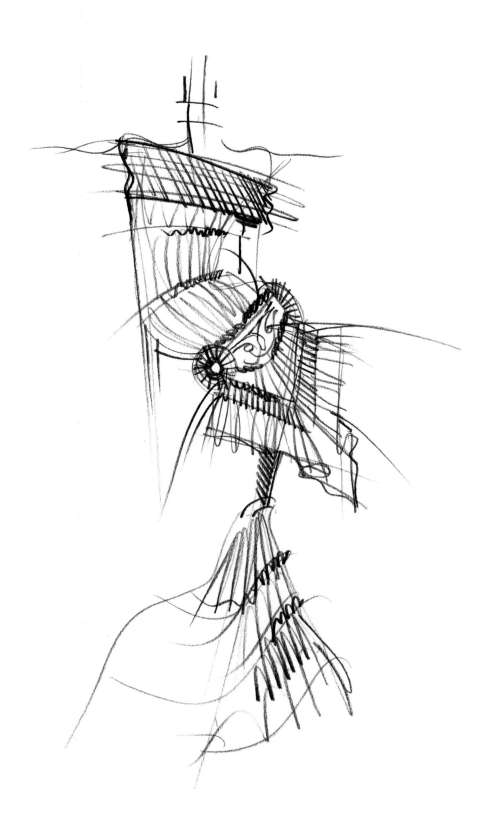

66 *On the evening of the ball Teresa was attired in her best, her most brilliant ornaments in her hair, and gayest glass beads — she was in the costume of the women of Frascati.*
Alexandre Dumas, *The Count of Monte Christo*

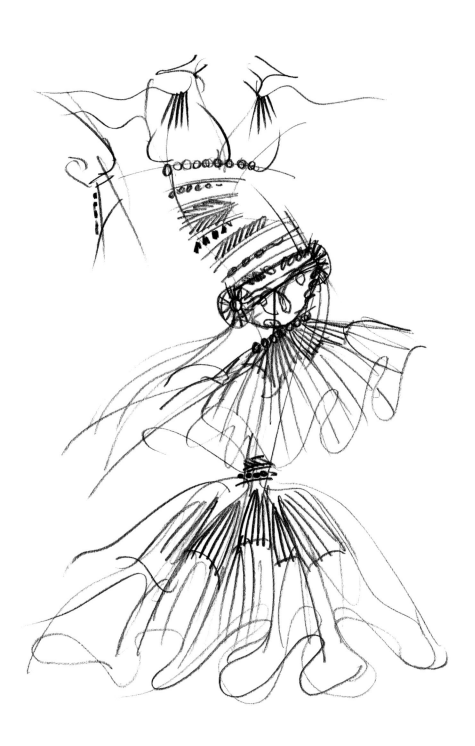

mistress of King Henry IV (who her husband Louis XVI came dressed as). Weber cites a description by the Marquis de Ségur. He describes her costume as "truly resplendent":

> A black hat, trimmed with white plumes held in place by four large diamonds and a loop of precious stones valued at 2,000 livres. Her stomacher and her girdle were made of diamonds, her dress was white gauze studded with silver stars, trimmed with golden fringe, which was attached to the skirt by more diamonds. A fairylike vision, indeed, but a ruinous one, from the point of view of the treasury.

The Queen's costume balls became much talked about and set fashion trends. Even those at court who did not particularly like her were won over by her fabulous costume parties. It did not take long for the social fashions of France to make their way across the Channel, where the English royalty embraced the continental masque. Not only did they enjoy masked balls, but in the style popularised by Catherine de Medici, they also staged court entertainments in which the nobility dressed in costume and performed in ballets, plays and pageants. The royals in attendance might also participate in dressing up and certainly in the dancing that followed.

The costume party demands flamboyance, as in the dramatic lines of Gianfranco Ferre's cape (opposite), John Galliano's stylised geisha dress for Christian Dior, (left) or Lloyd Klein's romantic, distressed ballgowns, featuring tightlaced bodices and tulle skirts (preceding pages).

England's Queen Anne, wife of King James I, was especially fond of the masque and from her seat at Somerset House, which she renamed Denmark House, staged many lavish entertainments in the early years of the seventeenth century. She commissioned Ben Johnson to write masques with roles for herself and other members of court. Sets and costumes were designed by Inigo Jones, and composers were commissioned to write the music. Putting on these events cost thousands of pounds, and one English commentator remarked that the court of James I was a "continual masquerade; the Queen and her ladies like so many sea nymphs or Nereid, appeared in various dresses, to the ravishment of the beholders."

Somerset House was also the setting for a revival of the masquerade ball, which had evolved from formal court entertainment to a party in which all participated. As was often the case with trends in fashion, food and lifestyle, the popularity of the masquerade ball in the royal courts of Europe spread to the public at large.

In *Masquerade and Civilisation*, Terry Castle explains the transition from the rarefied court masque. "Such aristocratic fantasia — the allegorical productions of Inigo Jones and others — probably had little direct impact on the popular resurgence of carnivalesque behaviour in the eighteenth century. The Jacobean masque was an expression of an elite aesthetic culture,

and a highly articulated, self-conscious artistic fantasy. It was a performance, and a performance for the few. In contrast, the eighteenth-century public masquerade … was an eminently unscripted unstaged event." In other words it was less connected with high culture and more to the popular carnival, where behaviour was more spontaneous and imbued with a sense of freedom.

Freedom, indeed, has always been at the heart of the masquerade. Putting on a mask, costume or disguise, immediately allows the wearer freedom to forget who they are and adopt another way of being, and behaving. That is all part of the appeal. In eighteenth-century England, the masquerade was an occasion when party-goers could lose their inhibitions. Wearing a disguise was imperative and half the fun of such events was trying to work out who was who, and flirting with everyone in the meantime. The ball might be a private affair, or offered for public subscription with tickets for sale.

A Swiss count by the name of John Heidegger is generally credited with making masquerade balls the height of fashion in London. He was an impresario, appointed as Master of Revels to King George II. He launched a series of parties for the well-to-do, which guests paid to attend. One of Heidegger's first masquerades was reported in detail by the *Weekly Journal* of February 15, 1718:

The Proust Ball, hosted in 1971 by Marie-Hélène Rothschild and her friend Baron Alexis de Redé for the centennial of the writer's birth, was the most talked-about party of the decade. Society photographer Cecil Beaton set up a makeshift studio to photograph some of the 800 guests, among them Elizabeth Taylor and Richard Burton.

The Room is exceedingly large, beautifully adorn'd and illuminated with 500 Wax Lights; on the Sides are divers Beauffetts, over which is written the several Wines therein contain'd, as Canary, Burgundy, Champaign, Rhenish, &c. each most excellent in its kind; of which all are at Liberty to drink what they please, with large Services of all Sorts of Sweetmeats. There are also two Setts of Musick, at due Distance from each other, perform'd by very good Hands. By the vast majority of Dresses (many of them very rich) you would fancy it a Congress of the principal Persons of all the World, as Turks, Italians, Indians, Polanders, Spaniards, Venetians, &c. There is an absolute Freedom of Speech without the least Offence given thereby; which all appear better bred than to offer at any Thing prophane, rude, or immodest; but Wit incessantly flashes about in Repartee, Honour, and good Humour, and all kinds of Pleasantry … The Number when I was there on Tuesday, last week, was computed at 700, with some Files of Musquetiers at Hand, for the preventing any Disturbance might happen by Quarrels, &c. so frequent in Venice, Italy, and other Countries, on such Entertainments.

By "Quarrels", we can well imagine what the writer might mean. As is often the case at parties, jealousy is a common cause of falling out and arguments. At a masquerade the potential for lover's quarrels is all the greater. Certainly seventeenth-century moralists believed that the masquerade encouraged licentiousness. Addison writing in *The Spectator* asserted that "the whole Design of this libidinous Assembly seems to terminate in Assignations and Intrigues." Another commentator of the time wrote in *The Guardian* that "being in disguise takes away

Two dresses by designer Zac Posen demonstrate his understanding of historical dress and costume, fostered during an internship at The Metropolitan Museum of Art's Costume Institute. Through drape, panelling and cut-outs, Posen's gowns strategically reveal and conceal to create dramatic impact, in the same way that the masks at a costume ball only partially disguise the wearer's identity.

"_Just around the corner in every woman's mind is a lovely dress, a wonderful suit, or entire costume which will make an enchanting new creature of her._

Wilhela Cushman

FRANCO
FERRE

Some of the most effective costumes in the history of the masquerade have relied on simplicity for their impact. The sinuous and revealing lines of Gianfranco Ferre's designs (left and opposite) bring to mind the much-published image of a young Penelope Tree arriving at Truman Capote's legendary Black and White Ball in a plain black catsuit with feline mask.

the usual checks and restraints of modesty; and consequently the beaux do not blush to talk wantonly, nor the belles to listen."

In his book *Masquerade and Civilisation: The Carnivalesque in Eighteenth Century Englisch Culture and Fiction*, Terry Castle points out that although "the masquerade was an established and ubiquitous feature of public life in England from the 1720s on, it was universally condemned by contemporary moralists and satirists as a foolish, irrational and corrupt activity perpetrated by irresponsible people of fashion ..."

Such criticism did nothing to dampen the public's love of the masquerade. "During the second and third decades of the century," writes Castle, "Count Heidegger's elaborate masquerades at the Haymarket drew up to a thousand antic "masks" weekly. Later, public masquerades at Vauxhall and Ranelagh, the Dog and Duck Gardens, Almack's, and the Pantheon, Mrs Cornley's extravaganzas at Carlisle House, and those prodigious costumed assemblies held in celebration of special events — the Jubilee of 1749, the King of Denmark's visit in 1768, the Shakespeare Jubilee of 1769 — attracted crowds numbering in the thousands." The rage for masked balls, whether private or public, continued for the best part of the century. The question of what to wear preoccupied the minds of many a fashionable Londoner. The wealthiest had costumes especially made to order. Those whose finances wouldn't stretch quite so far pored over newspapers for descriptions of the most elegant masquerades, and visited costume warehouses to purchase fancy dress designs. Some

masqueraders were more interested in what not to wear, or rather, wearing as little as they could get away with.

An infamous incident at a royal masquerade in 1749 involved the Queen's Maid of Honor, Miss Chudleigh, later Duchess of Kingston, who created quite a stir by attending as a bare-breasted Iphigenia. Reported one disgruntled guest, she was "so naked that the high priest might easily inspect the entrails of the victim." It helped preserve one's air of mystery on such occasions to be wearing a mask.

Of all the elements in the disguise, the mask is singled out for special attention. For many centuries the most important costume detail at the Venice carnival was, and still is, the mask. According to Castle, "it was the mask in particular, that indispensable element of masquerade disguise, that was thought most powerfully aphrodisiacal — for wearer and beholder alike." The author continues that, "At the same time, by a somewhat Proustian logic the mask was thought to heighten the desire of one's partner. The mask mystified the object of desire; it symbolised the absence or withholding of connection. It was a kind of stylised evasion — a formal sign of resistance to full human exchange. Not surprisingly, masked individuals were seen as fetishistically exciting." To make his point the author cites *The Country Wife*

Just like the masks worn at eighteenth-century masquerades, the hood can also function as a kind of aphrodisiac, concealing the wearer's identity to some extent yet also revealing tantalising glimpses. Giorgio Armani's glittering black dress mystifies the viewer by combining a hooded silhouette and revealing bodice.

(1675) by William Wycherley, in which the character of Pinchwife crudely observes that "A Woman mask'd is like a cover'd Dish, gives a Man curiosity, and appetite, when, it may be, uncover'd 'twould turn his stomach."

There are numerous references to masquerades in literature, perhaps because they provide ideal means for plot development. A masked ball features in some of Shakespeare's most notable plays, the perfect setting for employing the writer's favourite devices of mistaken identity and disguise. *Twelfth Night* and *Much Ado About Nothing* are examples. By the same token, literature has inspired some of the great costume balls. A popular trend of the masquerades of the nineteenth century was to dress as a famous character from a novel or drama.

One example is the costume ball hosted in 1826 by the British Ambassador to Vienna, Sir Henry Wellesley. It was intended to be such a lavish and memorable occasion that Sir Henry commissioned illustrators, writers and a publisher to produce a book celebrating the event. The book was rather grandly entitled: *From Characters in the Grand Fancy Ball given by the British Ambassador Sir Henry Wellesley at Vienna, at the conclusion of the Carnival, 1826; In Thirteen Highly Coloured Plates With A Description of the Entertainments On That Occasion.*

A masquerade disguise releases the wearer from a sense of personal duty and sets the scene for seduction. A mask can be literal, as in the leopard-print mask worn with fur by J Mendel (opposite) or created with the illusion of a wig and make-up (overleaf).

The introduction to the book trumpeted that:

On the last day but one of the Carnival, Sir Henry Wellesley, the British Ambassador, gave a grand costume-ball at his hotel in Vienna. It is universally admitted, that all the preceding entertainments of this kind which have taken place at Berlin, and in the Austrian capital, are not to be compared with this … the selection of the characters was most judicious: They were taken from the Novels of Sir Walter Scott and those of Baron La Motte Fouqué. *The Monastery, Kenilworth, Quentin Durward, The Crusaders,* and *Ivanoe* were the works of the Author of *Waverley*, the personages of which were conjured up into a magic like; and from the Romances of La Motte Fouqué were chosen *Udine, The Four Brothers of the Weserburg, The Magic Ring* and *The Lion Hunt. Libussa, Hamlet,* and a Polish quadrille concluded the whole. Between ten and eleven o'clock the company assembled, and the procession, arranged according to the quadrilles, began. It was an enchanting sight to see it moving through the brilliantly lighted apartments. The glistening of jewels and embroidery eclipsed the thousands of tapers, and the dazzled eye could scarcely endure the splendour arising from the union of the utmost magnificence and the highest elegance. The enlivening notes of a grand march accompanied the train; a page, as a herald, preceded each

quadrille; the name of the novel to which the characters belonged was displayed on a banner. Scott's *Monastery* opened the festive series. A herald and twelve masks formed this first quadrille.

The author notes that: "The archduchesses were resplendent with diamonds and jewels of immense value, which, united with the personal charms of those illustrious females, produced a truly magic effect." He singles out Her Imperial Highness the Archduchess Henrietta, dressed as Mary Stuart, Queen of Scots, and Her Imperial Highness the Archduchess Clementine, dressed as Catharine Seyton, for special comment: "The happy choice of the colours of the dresses added to the force of the impression; the dark waves of the black velvet in which the Queen of Scots was attired heightened by the dazzling brightness of the white diamonds which adorned her; and the light dress worn by Catharine Seyton combined with the brilliance of her jewels into an exquisite tout-ensemble."

Also notable was the character of Marie (from *The Lion Hunt* by Friedrich de la Motte Fouqué), who was played by Countess Esterhazy-Weissenwolf attired in Turkish pants under a calf-length white silk dress which was edged with blue embroidery and topped with a fur-trimmed cloak. At her neck she wore strings of diamonds, and an Eastern headwear,

Recalling the masquerading ladies of Marie Antoinette's French court, Ludmilla Tchérina attends a ball in 1966. A prima ballerina and star of The Red Shoes *she clearly understood the power of a good costume.*

a kind of turban with a pointed crown. On her feet were tiny gold pointed silk slippers.

A fascination with the "exotic" cultures of the East is a recurring theme of European masquerade balls. Oriental dress was often a feature of Venetian masquerade balls, and perhaps originated from the city's early history of trade with Asia. Lord Byron, in *Beppo: A Venetian Story*, describes the fashion at the Venetian costume ball thus:

> And there are dresses splendid, but fantastical,/Masks of all times and nations, Turks and Jews,/And harlequins and clowns, with feats gymnastical/Greeks, Romans, Yankee-doodles, and Hindoos;

At the famed ball given by Louisa, Duchess of Devonshire at her London home in 1897, to celebrate Queen Victoria's Diamond Jubilee, the hostess chose to dress as Zenobia, Queen of Palmyra. She had turned to Monsieur Worth in Paris for her costume, and the celebrated couturier had designed a magnificent dress made of silver tissue and gold cloth. She accessorised the gown with jewels worn from head to foot, and made a fantastic sight standing at the top of the marble staircase to welcome guests as they entered the house, accompanied by the strains of the Blue Hungarian Band in the entrance hall.

Some of the most strikingly attired guests also wore Oriental-inspired costume. A report of the event in *The Woman at Home* described some of the highlights in awed tones: "The Countess of Dudley wore a marvellous dress as Queen Esther, a mass of

IRINA

embroidery under a floating robe of peach gauze, with pale poppies and superb jewels almost covering her head … Of the beauties, the most conspicuous were Lady de Grey, a magnificent Cleopatra, Lady de Trafford, a too-lovely Semiramis, Mrs Jack Menzies as Titania, the Countess of Westmorland as Hebe, and the Duchess of Leeds as Lalla Rookh …" The account continued rapturously:

There were three Queen of Shebas, and Paris himself could scarcely have decided to which the apple of beauty should have been awarded. Lovely Lady Cynthia Graham was one, in white satin embroidered in gold and silver and bring rose. Princess Henry of Pless was another, and her dress was absolutely magnificent in its barbaric splendour of turquoise, emerald, amethyst, and ruby, caught in a web of finest gold, and spread thickly upon the dress and train of diaphanous gauze in purple and gold, its shifting light seeming to mingle with that of the jewels. Black attendants bore her train along, and among her girl attendants was her pretty sister, Miss Cornwallis West, in an Ethiopian dress of snowy crêpe, girdles with jewels

The fantastical designs of Italian couturiers Grimaldi Giardina appear tailor-made for a costume ball. In line and delicate decorative style they bring to mind the Belle Epoque, the decadent last years of the nineteenth century and first decade of the twentieth, when Paris was the setting for lavish parties almost every night of the week. The passion for dressing up was inspired by Leon Bakst's costumes for the Ballet Russes, which had become the sensation of Paris.

under a flowing rope of gold tissue. A drapery of gold and pink shot tissue was held around the hips by jewelled wings, and the pleated Liberty silk underdress was hemmed with pink roses, repeating the flowers in the hair.

The Duchess of Devonshire's Ball is remembered as one of the finest parties of that century. It starred a lavish setting, and even more fantastical costumery on which attendees had spent an estimated £500 a head. In her book *The Duchess of Devonshire's Ball*, Sophia Murphy reasons that "For all those who had attended the ball, the rest of the season's entertainments must have seemed very flat. As the preparations beforehand had been the chief topic of conversation in society, so was discussing the ball itself the main subject for many months afterwards, much to the chagrin, no doubt, of those who had not been invited."

All the newspapers and weekly magazines had covered the event in great detail, with headlines such as "The Duchess's Great Ball" and "Extraordinary Social Function". It was reported in the papers as far away as New York where it would have caught the attention of that city's most celebrated giver of costume parties, Alva Vanderbilt. In fact her daughter, Conseulo, had attended the Duchess of Devonshire's Ball.

The fashion for costume balls had already spread from Europe to New York some decades before, and the city's most prominent families vied to outdo one another. In particular Caroline Astor and Alva Vanderbilt became social rivals on a grand scale,

and the story of their war of resistance is part of New York lore. Caroline Astor was born into a wealthy merchant family descended from New York's first Dutch settlers. She married William Astor Jr. in 1853 and set about creating the "Four Hundred", a social list comprising a hand-picked group of upper class families. Left off the list, much to her resentment was Alva Vanderbilt, married to William Kissam Vanderbilt, the second richest man in America. Unfortunately for Alva, William's grandfather had crossed the Astors in a business dealing in 1867, and so Caroline was determined to lock Alva out of her elite company of four hundred.

However, Alva was not to be deterred. In 1883, to celebrate the building of a superb new house at 660 Park Avenue, she and William planned a house-warming party in the form of a fancy dress ball. Invitations to the Vanderbilt *bal a masque* duly went out to 1,200 of the most prominent members of New York society, all curious to see the magnificent new house. There was one notable exclusion from the invitation list; Caroline Astor was not invited.

"Society was torn between curiosity and betrayal," writes Alexis Gregory in her book *Families of Fortune: Life In the Gilded Age*, "until Caroline came home to find her excited daughter and friends rehearsing the quadrille they expected to dance … Blithely

The art of fashionable disguise is perfected in this feathered dress from Chanel's haute couture spring-summer 2007 collection, transforming the wearer into a rarefied avian beauty. Hundreds of feathers are individually applied to create an impression of volume.

assuming they would of course be invited, the girls had already settled on their dates. The author continues that "Caroline, unable to admit that an Astor daughter would not be welcome at the Vanderbilt party, dispatched a blue-liveried footman to deliver her card, corner turned down, to the Vanderbilts' maroon-liveried butler. Having thus broken the ice, she received back an invitation just in time to order herself a Venetian dress of dark-coloured velvet and satin sewn with solid gold roses and hundreds of seed pearls."

There was perhaps one other costume ball during New York's so-called "gilded age" that rivalled, at least in ostentation, even Alva Vanderbilt's. It was held by James Hazen Hyde, heir to the massive Equitable Life Assurance Society of New York. He spent most of his time living in France but in 1905 he decided to share his appreciation for French culture and finery with his American friends by throwing a costume party, themed "the court of Louis XVI", at Louis-Sherry's banqueting hall and ballroom. The guest of honour was French actress Gabrielle Réjane.

Alexis Gregory describes how the ballroom of Sherry's was transformed into a wing of Versailles, "with thousands of roses hung from lattices, screens, arbors, trellises, canopies and arches." She continues, "The assembled company rose grandly to the occasion. Mrs George Gould, daughter-in-law of the railroad robber baron, came dressed as Marie Antoinette, her green-velvet train lined in white satin and trimmed in real gold and emeralds. James Hazen Hyde arranged for the entire Metropolitan Opera orchestra and corps de ballet to provide entertainment until midnight. At that moment "Mme Réjane, dressed as a courtier, made her entrance on a sedan chair borne by four Nubian slaves." Guests then proceeded to another "wing of Versailles" for supper and afterwards danced until three in the morning. For those who lasted the distance, a breakfast of crab cakes and champagne was served at six in the morning. The ball was widely reported, with photographs of the richly costumed attendees appearing in all the newspapers. As the event was paid for by the life assurance society, shareholders were outraged and the government launched an investigation. It was not long before Hyde was on a ship bound for France, never to return.

The gilded era of decadent costume parties was almost at an end, but not before one final hoorah in the years leading up to the start of World War I. Interestingly, this final burst of fashionable parties was dominated by an obsession with the East.

The most celebrated example of the Oriental masquerade is Paul Poiret's Thousand-and-Second-Night ball held in 1911. He had determined to give a ball that would outdo any other, and settled on a luxurious Persian theme to which 300 guests were invited. His Paris showroom was transformed into

Photographer Slim Aarons, who charmed both Hollywood stars and the international jetset, found himself at the scene of some of the great parties of the 1950s and 1960s. In Los Angeles, Romanoff's Restaurant was often the setting for private celebrations, including this fancy dress party photographed in 1950.

a Persian palace, with tapestries draped over the windows and rugs on the floor to create the right effect. The dress code was strictly enforced. If, on arrival, guests were considered to be unsuitably attired, they were dispatched upstairs to change into a Persian outfit provided. If they refused they were sent home.

Once inside the "palace", guests could wander in the inner salon, transformed into a Persian courtyard with fountains and a blue and gold tent draped overhead. They would then find their way to the large gilded cage in which Poiret had "imprisoned" his "ladies of the harem", one of whom was Madame Poiret. Outside in the garden, monkeys, parrots and parakeets brought the scene to life, as did fortune tellers, an orchestra and a buffet laden with curries and Persian delicacies. Poiret had ensured the bar was well stocked, describing "a dusky bar where only the liquers were luminous. What alchemist had prepared the startling phantasmagoria of this disturbing laboratory ... A hundred long-necked carafes, a hundred crystal ewers contained all the beverages whose gamut extends from violet anisette and garnet bitters to emerald crème-de-menthe and golden citronella."

Eventually morning came and the guests departed. But just a day or so later there would be other fancy

Truman Capote spent three months working on the invitation list for his legendary Black and White Ball of 1966. Henry Fonda, who had been named by the New York Times as one of the elite "in crowd", and his wife Shirlee Mae Adams were among the first on Capote's list.

dress parties to attend and the social whirl would continue. After World War I, however, the mood changed. As James Laver writes: "The old leisure and much of the old elegance was gone, the pursuit of pleasure was a more hurried and hectic business, and there was nothing of the languorous odalisque in the short-skirted, cropped-haired, red-lipped charlestoning woman of the next decade."

However, not all was lost. New artistic movements, artists, designers, writers and personalities began to breathe life into the social scene on both sides of the Atlantic. Parties took on a less extravagant but more decadent tone, and amongst the popular forms of entertainment, the masquerade was revived.

Fashion historian Caroline Evans describes the role played by Elsa Schiaparelli in outfitting high society for the fashionable costume balls of the 1920s and 1930s, in her essay "Masks, Mirrors and Mannequins: Elsa Schiaparelli and the Decentred Subject". She writes: " … Schiaparelli both designed for, and attended, many of her clients' costume balls, such as Daisy Fellowes' Oriental Ball in 1935 … to which Schiaparelli went as a black Venetian page. The same year as Schiaparelli's Circus collection, Lady Mendl, another client of hers, gave a 'circus' party."

It makes sense that the Surrealist designer and her circle should find costume parties, or masquerades, the natural outlet for their artistic proclivities. The idea of the mask and the questioning of identity were key Surrealist concepts that were ideally suited to expression in the form of the masquerade. In spirit, the Surrealist balls seemed to capture the earthy exuberance of the early Venetian carnivals. Writing in *Women Artists and the Surrealists*, author Whitney Chadwick recounts how at one party, guests had to appear nude, but only between chest and thigh — the Surrealist artist Leonor Fini wore knee-length leatherette boots and a cape of white feathers. Max Ernst came kitted in a belt of iron spikes, a headdress and breastplate made from potscrubbers.

As Caroline Evans observes: "The huge popularity in the 1930s of masquerade parties and balls is testimony not only to the influence of popular Surrealism on fashion and social life but also to a contemporary concern with the surface of things. Schiaparelli's designs, and the fashions for masquerade balls of the 1930s, as well as Surrealist publications, parties and manifestos, can all be taken as a response to, but also a participation in, a growing sense of the instability of the modern world."

Perhaps the most talked about masquerade party, indeed any party, of modern times was Truman Capote's Black and White Ball. A celebration of Capote's success with *In Cold Blood*, and a diversion for the flamboyant writer who found himself with time to kill and money to spend, the ball was a lesson in how to throw a fabulous party. In her book, *Party of the Century*, Deborah Davis explains the background to Capote's grand ball: "The rich history of masked

Spain is the inspiration for Gianfranco Ferre's ensemble (opposite), while the Orient provided the theme for Paul Poiret's fancy dress design from 1911 (overleaf, left), worn to his party the same year, and for Sophia Loren's costume for her role in Lady L *in 1965 (overleaf, right).*

balls, filled with tales of success and failure, yielded several important lessons for any would-be party giver with ambitions as large as Truman's. From Elsa Maxwell he learned that the successful host did not have to be beautiful or wealthy, although it helped to have guests who were both. Arrivals and entrances needed to be staged, like a form of theater. When entertaining, even on a grand scale, less was more: one tasteful menu was preferable to twenty-eight courses, yet two orchestras were always better than one. Members of the press needed to be embraced; with their help — and headlines — a party could live in legend. Every host needed that all-important gimmick, a theme to make his or her party stand out from the rest. Truman's answer was to hold a Black and White Ball, and every guest, no matter how rich or famous, must come hidden behind a mask."

In deciding on a masked ball, Capote virtually guaranteed that his ball would be one of the most talked-about events of the decade, yet he may not have envisioned that it would, some fifty years later, be referred to as "the party of the century". It was not because the costumes were particularly lavish or expensive; in many cases they were rather simple — Penelope Tree wore a black catsuit while Mia Farrow wore a sleeveless white shift. It was the personalities that made it special, the exclusive nature of the occasion, and most importantly, the insistence that every guest wear a mask.

Anna Molinari's showgirl (opposite) references the circus, a recurring theme at fashionable costume parties of the 1920s and 1930s. Grimaldi Giardina's dress (left) recalls the Renaissance with its exaggerated lines.

Chapter Two

The Formal Party

"Not even the most beautiful ballroom in the world, decorated like the Garden of Eden, could in itself suggest a brilliant entertainment, if the majority of those who filled it were frumps.

Emily Post, Etiquette (1922)

The idea of dressing up in special clothing for special occasions is as old as civilisation. In particular, dressing up to snare a mate is a long-running theme in social history. Women typically dressed to showcase their finest features at dances and feasts that gave parents, especially royalty and the wealthy, the chance to display their daughters. It is no coincidence that the heroines of so many fictional works of the eighteenth and nineteeth centuries invariably caught the eye of some suitor at a ball attended during the social season.

The ball is not the only kind of formal event. There is the dinner party, which although these days can be an informal affair, was until the last few decades at least, almost always very much an occasion with a dress code. In her classic book of advice for the fashionable woman, *A Guide to Elegance*, published in 1964, Genevieve Antoine Dariaux found it necessary to spell out the intricacies of dinner party dressing: "When you are invited to a dinner party it is always a good idea to inquire as to the number of guests as well as to the degree of formality of the occasion. Usually, if it is a black-tie dinner, your hostess will send you a written invitation bearing the notation 'black-tie' in the corner, you then will know that you are expected to dress in evening clothes, either long or short."

Black and white has long been the classic, and failsafe, dress code for a formal event. In this fashion photograph from the 1950s, Cecil Beaton captures the epitome of the look: a black gown, décolloté, with emphasis on pale shoulders and a tiny waist. Jewellery is sparkling but discreet, hair is swept up into a chignon, and lips and nails are red.

Here, Madame Dariaux makes a deliberate distinction between the two main types of formal attire for women, the dinner dress and the balldress. Dinner dresses, she cautions, should be far less elaborate. "The most elegant are, of course, floor-length, either with sleeves and a low-cut neckline, or sleeveless with a high neckline, and they can be just as well made of wool as of silk. Short dinner dresses require a richer material, or even beaded embroidery," advises Madame Dariaux, who as directrice at Nina Ricci for many years had excellent fashion sense.

She also doled out good advice on how to smoothly navigate a course to social acceptance. "When the men are asked to wear dark business suits you can confidently slip into your low-cut little black crepe dress, for you can be sure that is exactly what all the other women are going to do," she offers as one safe option. The advice continues, on a more hopeful note. "If this prospect seems simply too dreary (and I can understand how you feel), an evening suit of velvet or brocade in a bright colour in the winter, and of lace or a crisp lustrous silk in a pastel colour in the summer, would be quite appropriate, while a low-cut sheath of white wool or crepe is perfect during any season of the year." Naturally, other types of formal parties can include a dinner. But an invitation to a dinner party is really only just for dining, not dancing or entertainment.

Emily Post, the early twentieth-century authority on dress and manners, distinguished between dinner dresses and balldresses, pointing out that with a balldress, freedom of movement for dancing was the main consideration:

A dinner dress really means every sort of low, or half low evening dress. A formal dinner dress, like a balldress, is always low-necked and without sleeves, and is the handsomest type of evening dress that there is ... The perfect balldress is one purposely design with a skirt that is becoming when dancing. A long wrapped type of dress would make Diana herself look like a toy monkey on a stick, but might be dignified and beautiful at dinner. A dinner dress differs from a balldress in little except that it is not necessarily designed for freedom of movement.

Prior to the eighteenth century, the style of a formal dress was far less important than the fabric it was made from. Textiles were an important signifier of wealth. Therefore the clothes that were worn in public sent an instantaneous message about the wearer's finances. Historian Sue Vincent writes that for people of some social standing in seventeenth-century England clothing was "a key determinant of economic identity. Again and again when seeking to make their pecuniary position clear, it was the sartorial state they described." She cites the 1676 memoirs of Lady Ann, wife of the diplomat Sir Richard Fanshawe, who served under Charles I and Charles II. In one particular episode, when her belongings

Formal gowns typically fall into two camps: the grand balldress, which emphasises volume and clearly separates the bodice and skirt with a small waist; and the fitted chemise dress which follows the body more closely as does this 1930s-inspired dress by J Mendel. It emphasises the height of the wearer by creating one unbroken line.

were stolen on a sea voyage, Lady Ann makes clear the value of her fine clothing. The thieves had stolen "a bag of 60lb and a quantity of gold lace, with our best clothes and linnin and all my combs, gloves and ribonds, which amounted to near three hundred pounds more."

The same year that Lady Ann wrote her memoirs, Lady Chaworth also wrote hers under the title *Belvoir Castle Calendar*. Commenting on the value of formal dress she wrote that "the clothes last night at the Queenes birth-night ball was infinite rich, especially Mis Phraser, who put downe all for a gowne, black velvet, imbroydered with all sorts of slip inbost worke of gold and silver, and peticote one broad ernine and gold lace all over; yet I do not aprove the fancy of either, though they say cost £800."

Parties were not only a great opportunity for guests to show off their finery, but, just as importantly, they enabled the host to display his or her wealth and taste. One of the great show-offs of the seventeenth century was Nicolas Fouquet, who threw a party of great splendour purely to impress the King of France, Louis XIV. It was also intended to win back the favour of the King and ensure his political survival. Fouquet was a high-ranking civil servant, appointed Superintendent of Finance to the King in 1653. He had made a fortune through various means, including skimming vast funds from the state bankroll. He used his money to build a magnificent chateau, Vaux le Vicomte, which rivalled even the King's palace. Although Fouquet had done his best to keep prying eyes away from the building site, the King's court had plenty of resourceful spies happy

to turn the King against the ruthless but brilliant Fouquet. Rumours flew around the court about where he had managed to get so much money, and everyone including the King was curious to see the results of the huge expenditure.

Although somewhat out of favour in recent times, brightly coloured formal gowns have enjoyed great popularity in the past. Examples here are a yellow dress from the early 1950s (opposite), when festive colour was considered more youthful and fashionable than black or white, and Lanvin's violet dress from the 1930s (below).

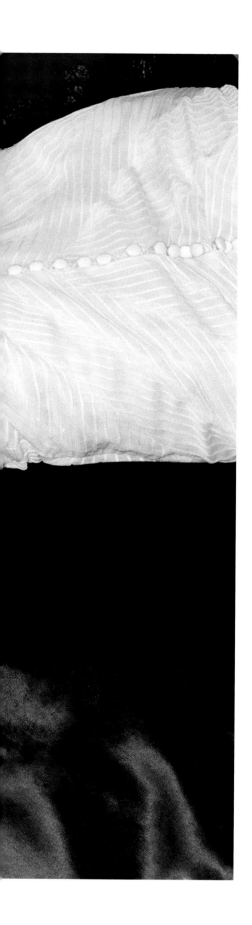

An exaggerated shoulder has been a recurring style in formal evening dress, as shown here in the portrait of Nina Ricci (below) and a contemporary design by J Mendel (left). The look was especially popular in the 1930s, when one large shoulder decoration was typically used on an otherwise streamlined design. The device was used by designers in that decade, and again in the 1980s, to emphasise the wearer's height and make hips seem narrower.

The shape of the classic ball gown has not changed for centuries. Essentially it comprises a very fitted bodice and a full skirt. Slim sleeves may be inset as in Escada's sapphire-blue dress (opposite), a popular style in the early Victorian period because it emphasised the wearer's delicacy. Another variation is a décolloté, off-the-shoulder neckline, as in Ferre's black gown (left), an innovation of the 1640s.

A successful party dress reveals only part of the body, whether shoulders (above), legs (opposite), or back (overleaf), as evident in George Barbier's 1920 lithograph in which a man is entranced by the sight of a bare back.

To make matters worse, during the construction of the costly chateau, Fouquet had attempted to win the attnetions of a beautiful courtier, who everyone knew was already the object of affection of Louis himself. Realising he was in serious jeopardy, Fouquet thought of a way out. He would quickly finish off the chateau and throw a party for the entire court, with the King as guest of honour. Perhaps he had in mind the words written by one of the authorities of the time on refined cookery, who wrote under the initials L.S.R.: "The beauty of a meal is infinitely greater in the evening, by torchlight, than during the day, and one even eats better, for when business affairs have been put at a slight distance, and when the number of intrusions have diminished, one is naturally destined to discover the sweeter pleasures of life." Fouquet gambled that a dinner party on a lavish scale would so indulge and entertain the King that the all-powerful royal would overlook the indiscretions of his Finance Superintendent and restore him to a favoured position in the court.

Indulged the King certainly was. Fouquet's party, held on August 17, 1661, was on such an incredible scale that it is impossible to calculate the cost. The entire French court was invited — one estimate of the time put the guest list at more than 6,000. The proceedings began at 6pm when a gilded carriage arrived carrying Louis XIV, his brother and three of his favourite court ladies. Once all the guests were assembled, the evening commenced with a stroll through the sweeping terraced gardens, which were exquisitely designed with lawns, scrolling hedges and flowerbeds, fountains and sculptures. The king and his mother were presented with diminutive canopied

〜〜 *The late nineteenth century lived up to its name as "The Gilded Age". Charles Frederick Worth's evening gown of 1898 (above) captures the elaborate yet refined sensibility of that period, with an art nouveau scroll design in black silk velvet on a background of heavy white satin. Decades later the white satin gown, albeit with more delicate decoration, remained a staple in the wardrobes of society women. The Wyndham Sisters (opposite), Mrs John Wyndham, Lady Cranborne, and Lady Roderic, posed for this photographic portrait in 1950, styled after the painter John Singer Sargent.*

carriages, narrow enough to navigate the garden paths. The rest of the court followed behind on foot, attired in high heels and brilliant coloured silks adorned with ribbons and feathers. Everyone had been eagerly anticipating the event and had spent weeks planning their outfits. Gondolas ferried the guests across a wide canal to the grotto, from where they could admire the full sweep of the gardens and the imposing chateau beyond.

Dinner at the chateau was served in the grand salon, where guests marvelled as thousands of candles flickered into life, reflecting off Venetian mirrors, silk wall coverings, silver plates and crystal carafes, not to mention the costly diamond jewels worn by the ladies of the court. Once guests were seated, the cavalcade of dishes began arriving. There is no record of exactly what was eaten, but according to Carolin C. Young in her book *Apples of Gold in Settings of Silver*, the taste of the times would have dictated that they begin with potages of turkey, chicken with chicory, and stuffed quail: "These would be surrounded by entrees such as hashes of mushroom and artichokes, fricassees, boiled or stewed meats, and savoury pigeon tarts, two per potage. Plates of delicate hors d'oeuvres formed a border placed 'outside of the work'. The anonymous 1662 *L'Escole Parfaite des Officier de Bouche* suggests pâtés, foie gras, sausages, figs, raspberries, radishes, and hot venison pastry."

The second course would typically have comprised twenty to thirty roasts, a mix of rare game, lamb and beef, served with accompanying sauces, followed by more delicate roasts and rare birds. Then came entremets, delicacies such as truffles, pigeon wings,

pigs' ears, meat pastries, asparagus and artichokes, and no doubt green peas, newly introduced from Italy and the height of fashion at dinner parties, especially when served with English butter. The King ate with gusto, using his hands, as was the habit of France in that era. Only Fouquet chose to eat with a fork, adopting the Italian custom that would soon become widespread.

Dessert was the highlight of the feast, intended as one cookbook of the day put it, "to bait the appetite and spark thirst." During the final course "the spirit revives, the wittiest words are spoken, the most agreeable topics debated … it is then that the funniest stories are told … as they say, between the pear and cheese, a thousand pleasantries are invented to pass the time and entertain good company, which provide the greatest charm in life."

Fouquet's dessert course would have included some of the rare varieties of fruit grown in his garden, along with pears, figs, apricots, cherries and melons, grapes and sugared fruits, as well as richly coloured marzipans, pastries and cakes fashioned into shapes of flowers and birds. Accompanying the entire meal were fine chilled wines (the chateau had its own ice vault), including the King's favourite wine from Champagne (the still variety, as sparkling had not yet been invented).

The stole, or shawl, is an important accessory for formal occasions, particularly when a dress is strapless or off the shoulder. Shawls, especially those from Cashmere, became immensely popular in the early 1800s, when evening dresses were made of light, semi-sheer fabrics. The ability to wear a shawl elegantly was considered quite an accomplishment.

After dinner Fouquet led his guest of honour to an outdoor amphitheatre to see the performance of a special new production written specially for the occasion by Molière — *Les Fâcheaux*, the world's first comedy-ballet. A breathtaking display of fireworks then marked the close of the party. The King was delighted, but would it be enough to save Fouquet? Apparently not. Despite his last-ditch effort to resurrect his relationship with the King, Fouquet was arrested three weeks after the party and charged with treason and embezzlement. He was eventually sentenced to life imprisonment. Louis, meanwhile, had been so inspired by the evening at Fouquet's that he began planning his own magnificent grounds, the much-lauded gardens of Versailles.

Although Fouquet had used the setting of a vast dinner party to win the favour of the King, dinner parties are typically on a far more intimate scale, and often with far more romantic connotations. "Dinner makes a perfect first date," writes Carolin C. Young. "What other activity, except for sexual intercourse itself, is as intimate, as voluptuously sensuous, and as engagingly tactile as a shared meal? Why else would so many conservative cultures such as those of Arabs and Orthodox Jews, ban seating the sexes together at tables outside of the family setting?"

It is at the small intimate dinner party that dress takes on even more importance than usual. Rather than impressing with wealth or status, the dress is intended to seduce. What intimate dinner party can compare with that held by Casanova and a mystery woman in Venice in 1753? Casanova had received an anonymous invitation while in church. The

In place of a shawl or cape, an evening coat can transform an apparently simple dress into something more polished. English couturiers Robinson Valentine pair a black, flower-trimmed coat with a long white dress (opposite). For red-carpet events, however, no wrap or covering should detract from the impact of the dress. Strapless beaded and ruched gown (below) by Luca Luca.

invitation read: "A nun, who has seen you every feast day for the past two months and a half in the church of her convent wishes to make your acquaintance." It was signed with the initials M.M. Although somewhat stunned by the forward nature of the invitation, Casanova was intrigued and readily agreed to meet the nun at the designated place: a luxurious *pied à terre* on the island of Murano, gracefully decorated in the French Rococo style. The occasion was to be an intimate supper, or *souper intime*.

Casanova's admirer was waiting for him. As he describes her, "about twenty-two or twenty-three ... a perfect beauty, tall, white of complexion as to verge on pallor, with an air of nobility and decision but at the same time of reserve and shyness, large blue eyes; a sweet, smiling face, beautiful lips damp with dew." She was not dressed in her nun's habit but rather in the sophisticated style of an aristocratic woman in pale silks with lace ruffles, ribbons, jewels, and with hair pulled back in a chignon. Casanova fell to his knees to kiss her hands. Despite his best efforts to seduce, M.M. was intent on delaying the moment. After an hour or two of groping and pleading, and stealing kisses, the young woman announced that she was hungry. According to Carolin C. Young in her account of their meeting, "She proposed an impromptu supper, which in reality, had been as meticulously planned as any formal banquet. Gifted players at *souper intime* cultivated this fiction, essential to the spirit of romance."

A servant laid a table for two, with damask tablecloth and beautiful porcelain. The supper dishes were brought to a second serving table, and placed on silver boxes, filled with hot water to keep the food warm. Casanova does not record exactly what comprised the eight delicate supper courses, but there are other examples to indicate what would have been served on such an occasion.

The idea was not to eat heavy rich food that might bloat the stomach, but rather to enjoy light morsels aimed at stimulating desire. At a later supper hosted by Casanova he served sturgeon, truffles, small game and oysters. Casanova loved oysters. One story has it that he once seduced two young convent girls at a supper that began with one hundred oysters. Casanova also had a reputation for tossing oysters down the cleavage of his lover's dress, with the fun of retrieval in mind.

Casanova adored women with appetites and few things made him more aroused than watching a woman eat. He had come up with his own theories that certain flavours matched certain types of women. Blondes should eat delicate cheeses, greens and fish cooked in butter; brunettes peppered salami, stewed game, strongly coloured vegetables, and pungent cheese; and redheads a combination of sweet and spicy foods to match their pale skin and supposedly fiery temperament.

Jacqueline and Caroline Lee Bouvier (later Jacqueline Kennedy/Onassis, and Princess Lee Radziwill), photographed at a ball in 1951, the same year Jacqueline met John F. Kennedy. Three years earlier at the age of eighteen she had been named "Queen Deb of the Year" by Hearst gossip columnist Igor Cassini (brother of designer Oleg), who described her as "a regal brunette who has classic features and the daintiness of Dresden porcelain."

At Casanova's supper of seduction with the mysterious M.M. he was aroused by the sight of the beautifully dressed nun consuming her food with gusto. It was not just the vision of her eating that Casanova found so alluring, it was also the fact that M.M., a nun, was here attired as an aristocratic beauty in a frivolous silk dress adorned with ribbons and bows. Alas, his passion was not to be sated that evening — M.M. prolonged that pleasure by making him wait until their next supper date.

These suppers, although not strictly formal, serve as an example of the importance of dressing for dinner. The beautifully feminine rustling silks worn by M.M. for her assignation with Casanova, were in the style made fashionable by the influential Madame de Pompadour, the quintessential style icon of the French Rococo period. A courtesan and mistress to the French King Louis XV, she made it her mission to be the most captivating woman in the court. Dressing for dinner, as well as numerous other occasions consumed the best part of the day, as well as vast sums of money from the King's purse. For a woman with no real political power or security, Pompadour used her great style and fashion prowess to make herself virtually synonymous with the Rococo age, and firmly entrench her position as one of the most important figures in the court of King Louis. Even before Marie Antoinette, Madame de Pompadour was the ultimate party girl of the French court.

Into the life of a bored Louis XV, she brought parties, balls, masquerades, theatre performances and more. In fact they had first met at the ball given in honour of the King's wedding to Maria-Theresa of Spain. At that time, the woman who would become known as "The Pompadour" was Madame Lenormand d'Etoiles, the wife of a wealthy bureaucrat. She circled flirtatiously around the King for a while, and having caught his attention she dropped her silk handkerchief in front of him, accompanied by a come-hither glance, but she did not stop. The King, entranced, retrieved the handkerchief and came after her, having to reach over the crowds of party-goers to hand it back to her. Within a matter of weeks she was installed at Versailles as the Marquise de Pompadour.

Madame de Pompadour knew the true power of clothes and her whole process of dressing became a formality in itself. It was the custom at Versailles for courtiers to attend the levees, or morning toilette, of the King, and women of high society likewise often invited their friends to attend their own levees to help while away the hours spent at the dressing table. "The Pompadour" was masterful at using the occasion to wield power. In *The Elegant Woman*, author Gertrude Aretz describes Madame de Pompadour's routine:

> At her levees she was capable of advising ministers, disposing of high diplomatic posts, and sending out letters *de cachet*

The origins of the debutante ball can be traced to 1780 when the English King George III staged a ball for his wife Queen Charlotte. The tradition of a young woman's "coming out" continues in modern form in many countries, but few deb balls can compare with the Bal à la Haute Couture held at the Hotel de Crillon in Paris every year. Making her debut there in 2000, Lauren Bush wore a romantic haute couture gown from the atelier of Christian Dior.

from her boudoir, while all the time inflaming the senses of the King and her other admirers. She loved to prolong her levees as much as possible trying on every imaginable negligee, court dress, shoe, slipper, stocking, and garter. Every physical charm was brought into play in turn, for she was a true child of her period and professed the cult of her own beauty … The eyes of the men rested in admiration, and those of the few women present in curiosity, on this capricious ruler of elegance; but every woman observed carefully all the details of her clothes in order to copy them, until at last there was scarcely a single object, not a garment, not a piece of furniture, that was not à la Pompadour.

The King's mistress developed variations on a theme, designed to enhance her limited beauty. She made great use of silk in pastel shades, especially blues and pinks, and her party dresses with their wide crinoline skirts were adorned with ribbons, bows and floral motifs. The bodices of her dresses were cut low and square to show off her cleavage. She wore her hair swept up into a front roll, studded with gems; indeed her elaborate hairstyles developed into a signature look, taken even further by Marie Antoinette. Despite attempts to slavishly copy her style, Madame de Pompadour stayed ahead of the pack. Writes

Gertrude Aretz: "When she appeared during the last period of her reign, in the King's salon or at court festivities, where many young, beautiful and elegant women were present, and where she might well have feared competition, all eyes centred on her, although she was young and beautiful no longer. It is true that, in spite of all her despairing efforts, the decline of her charms was obvious enough, but her general appearance and bearing seemed to command: 'Look at me! Here I am!'"

The Pompadour had developed a distinct look, characterised by soft, flattering colours and feminine details. She was particularly adept at utilising accessories, without which the formal ensemble of the eighteenth-century was not complete. Fans, slippers, gloves, handkerchiefs and bags all took on a crucial role in aiding a woman's sense of elegance, and her ability to flirt. After all, without her handkerchief Madame de Pompadour might not so easily have won an encounter with the King. In this perhaps her only other rival of the age could be Marie Antoinette.

Of her yearly clothing allowance of 120,000 livres, the young Queen spent almost all of it on accessories. In Antonia Fraser's biography of Marie Antoinette, the author notes that eighteen new pairs of perfumed gloves and four pairs of shoes were ordered every week. It goes without saying that the clothing allowance was well and truly exceeded each year. The

The woman who wears a red dress makes a bold statement. The colour is associated with female sexuality and seduction, and also with wealth and privilege. Valerie Steele notes in her book, The Red Dress, *that "throughout recorded history, the high cost of producing red dyes meant that red clothing was only worn by those with power and status."*

Queen changed at least three times a day, and she rarely wore a dress more than once. The final change of the day was perhaps the most important — into a gala gown for the evening's formal entertainments at the palace, or for a trip to the Opera, or to the Opera Ball, in Paris.

Unlike Madame de Pompadour, Marie Antoinette was the Queen, and she was not so much copied for reasons of fashion, perhaps, as to remain in royal favour. As Caroline Weber writes in *Queen of Fashion*, "The women of the aristocracy … were too focused on keeping up with the Queen's ever-changing styles to question either their appropriateness or their cost. Whereas under previous monarchs, eminence of lineage, conformity to etiquette, and service to the crown had served as the nobility's chief arms of distinction, the nobles in Marie Antoinette's newly fashion-oriented court found that modishness represented a surer path to royal favour."

However, in some areas Marie Antoinette's style had a more profound effect on fashionable dressing than can be put down to politics. When she discovered the joys and simplicities of "pastoral" life, she was instrumental in ushering in a new rustic style of dress, even for parties. Gone were the crinolines, lavish coloured silks, powdered wigs. In their place were simple shifts in white or ivory, or pretty floral prints, often semi-transparent, with little adornment other than a broad sash, lace trim or other delicate touches.

Despite the simplified dress, she still managed to spend twice her yearly clothing allowance. Even after Marie Antoinette returned to more formal styles of dress, the new style continued to be all the rage in Paris, and beyond. At parties and balls, women accessorised their thin chemises with warm shawls in expensive cashmere and silk.

Across the Channel in England, one woman is considered responsible for introducing the French fashions to London society, in particular the simple muslin dress, which was even worn for the most formal of functions. Georgiana, Duchess of Devonshire was highly influential in shaping the tastes of the day. In her biography of the Duchess, Amanda Foreman explains that Marie Antoinette had sent a present to Georgiana of a muslin chemise with fine lace. "Taking advantage of the warm weather Georgiana made one of her most successful entrances when she arrived at the Prince of Wales' ball wearing white muslin decorated with silver sprigs," writes the author. "Soon the *Kady's Magazine* was claiming that 'all the Sex now, from 15 to 50 and upwards … appear in their white muslin frocks with broad sashes.'"

In modern times, the ball has become something of a rarity. Contemporary life is more casual, and the role of women is different. In ages past the ball served as one of the main arenas in which to meet a suitable gentlemen, or rather to be introduced to one, at least amongst the well-to-do.

Five couture ball gowns designed in 1951 by Jacques Fath. Carmel Snow, then editor of Harper's Bazaar, *once said of the French designer, "He makes you look like you have sex appeal — and believe me, that's important."*

The strapless line has dominated formal dress since the 1940s. Models wait backstage for a Jacques Fath haute couture show in 1942 (above), while Rita Hayworth, dubbed "The Best Dressed Girl in Hollywood", is resplendent in a white gown with feathered bodice (opposite), designed by costumer Gwen Wakeling for the 1942 film My Gal Sal.

It is impossible to count how many balls have been arranged and attended over the past several hundred years, how many beautiful gowns have been ordered and fitted for the occasion. But there are some events that have been special enough to catch the attention of historians. Costume historian James Laver maintained that "it is almost impossible to find a ball more celebrated than that given by the Duchess of Richmond on the eve of Waterloo." It was not the grandest of balls but it had atmosphere and character aplenty.

Held in Brussels on June 15, 1815, the Waterloo Ball was quite impromptu, thrown by the Duchess of Richmond when she heard the plight of officers stationed in the city awaiting their orders. The officers had requested an evening's entertainment outside the city but their commanders had refused on the grounds it would be a security risk. The Duchess heard about their disappointment and stepped in, offering to give them a party in a converted coach house in the Rue de la Blanchisserie. Former coach house it may have been but it was a very well appointed venue. There was a sizable ballroom, a billiard room and a dining room, as well as a study used by the Duke of Richmond.

A painting of the event by Robert Alexander Hillingford shows an elegant room hung with crystal chandeliers and draped with tapestries in the royal colours of crimson, gold and black. The officers look dashing in their red coats and cream breeches, and the women look dainty dressed in the simple ivory-coloured dresses of the Regency period. Remarkably, one of the gowns from the night survived, and is now displayed in England's Saffron Walden Museum. It is a delicate garment made from cream silk net, with garlands of flowers featuring on the bodice and around the hem. The short puffed sleeves are trimmed with silk chenille. Although simple, it is luxurious in its detail and fabric, and would fit beautifully in Hillingford's scene. Guests were piped in by the Scottish brigade and enjoyed a splendid evening with dancing, fine wines and dinner. Apart from the officers, the invitation list read like a roll call of European royalty and aristocracy. Among those in attendance were the Prince of Orange, Prince of Nassau, Duc d'Arenberg, Duc et Duchesse de Beaufort et Mademoiselle, Earl and Countess of Conyngham, Lord and Lady John Somerset, and, most famously, the Duke of Wellington.

Many years later, in 1890, the young daughter of the Duke and Duchess, Sarah, later Lady de Ros, wrote about that night for *Murray's Magazine*, recalling that "When the Duke [of Brunswick] arrived, rather late, at the ball, I was dancing, but at once went up to him to ask about the rumours. He said very gravely, 'Yes, they are true; we are off tomorrow.' This terrible news was circulated directly, and while some of the officers hurried away, others remained at the ball, and actually had not time to change their clothes, but fought in evening costume … It was a dreadful evening, taking leave of friends and acquaintances, many never to be seen again."

Sophia Loren, radiant in a strapless gown of lace and tulle, on the red carpet at the 8th Cannes International Film Festival in May 1955, the year the Palme D'Or award was introduced as the festival's highest honour. Six years later Loren would win Best Actress for La Ciociara.

black lace

peach starched chiffon

Bill Blass
3618 Calhoun St.
Fort Wayne, Ind.

Then twenty-three years old, Lady Sarah was deeply affected by the emotions of the evening, not least of all because she had fallen in love that night with Peregrine Maitland, commander of the 1st brigade of the Foot Guards. Like the other officers, he left the ball to meet Napoleon's troops at Quatre Bras. Happily for Lady Sarah he returned from war and the couple married a few months later (eloping to Paris due to the Duke's disapproval).

Not all the officers made it back. Of the ninety-four who had attended the ball, three died at the battle of Quatre Bras the following day, eight died at Waterloo three days later. Two more died of their wounds and at least thirty-six were wounded. Even Lord Byron was moved to pen homage to the ball, writing:

> There was a sound of revelry by night
> And Belgium's capital had gather'd then
> Her Beauty and her Chivalry
> And bright The lamps shone o'er fair
> women and brave men;
> A thousand hearts beat happily; and when
> Music arose with its voluptuous swell,
> Soft eyes look'd love to eyes which spake
> again,
> And all went merry as a marriage bell;
> But hush! Hark! A deep sound strikes like
> a rising knell!
> Did ye not hear it?

Not many balls can claim such historical significance nor conjure up such a sense of poignancy. While formal events such as the Waterloo Ball provided an ideal setting for romance, they were also an important

showcase for the fashions of the time. Women loved to compare the latest styles and gossip about who was wearing what. Eugenie Foa, writing in *Livres des Cent et Un* in 1886, advised: "The woman of fashion

The formal gown can also be romantic. An early Bill Blass design (opposite) featured a black lace bolero over a peach chiffon gown. For Mia Farrow, pictured in Frank Sinatra's townhouse in 1968 (below), Pierre Cardin created a cascading organza dress trimmed with silk flowers.

arrives at the ball; in alighting from her carriage, she is engaged to dance; on the staircase she is engaged, on the landing she is engaged; she was engaged the previous evening, the evening before that, at the last ball; she has more invitations on entering the room than she will dance quadrilles the whole night long … She remains a short time at the ball, as a flash of lightning, the time to dazzle, and then away; the same effect is repeated at two other balls; she departs, returns home in good time, long before fatigue and dancing have deadened the brightness of her eyes, uncurled her hair, taken the shine off her dress. She must have it said of her: 'She only came for an instant, she has so many invitations, so many duties of society to fulfil! One caught a sight of her with difficulty; but never did she look so pretty!'"

French women could rely on a wonderfully detailed source of fashion information in the form of Mallarmé's paper, *La Dernière Mode*. Although it was only published for a few years, it remains a rich reminder of the intricacies of late nineteenth-century dress codes, and the fact that dressing to impress was paramount.

As the authors of *Mallarmé on Fashion*, P.N. Furbank and A.M. Cain, write, "All social life in Paris is spectacle … The great entertainment consists in looking and in being looked at." And, for women in particular, "it should be remembered that it was the wife's duty to reflect her husband's wealth." This was

as true at a café, on holiday, at the theatre, and or course at the formal party.

In the November 15, 1874 issue of the paper, fashion writer Madame Marguerite de Ponty dispensed advice on the ball gown and its appropriate incarnation for that winter season:

> First and sole rule: Whilst the classic materials of ball gowns aim to envelop us in a fleeting mist, of a hundred shades of white, the dress itself, on the contrary — both the bodice and the skirt — is moulded more closely than ever to the body, a delightful and scientific opposition between the vague and the (of necessity) definite … To this sole, or at least first, rule … I add the two or three details, diverse but not contradictory.
>
> 1. Silk skirts are no longer made with puffs for eveningwear but are frilled at the top, and the frill is repeated five or six times (covering a space of about thirty centimetres). As for trimming, at the foot of the garment there should be flounces or gathers and further up (very much further up) there should be gauze scarves, set very high over the apron and secured to the train by a bow.
> 2. Waists are made with little rounded basques, or else points resembling basques

A dress that says "I've arrived" is what many party guests aspire to. By the 1950s, when this high fashion photograph was taken by Cecil Beaton, manufacturing techniques and materials meant that even a woman on a budget could indulge in a glittering, beaded and sequinned creation for a very modest price.

... A thousand exquisite combinations, familiar or quite new, may spring to the imagination of a Reader impatient for the first ball of winter; but the very choice of a material to send to the dressmaker is too intimately bound up with these for us to separate them.

Madame de Ponty goes on to describe the fabrics to employ in making these new styles, taking pains to differentiate between dresses for girls and dresses for young women. For ladies she recommends satin or faille veiled with white tulle and decorated with flowers at one side. Alternatively, dresses might be trimmed with real feathers, Brussels lace or *point d'Alençon* lace.

At the conclusion of several hundred words setting out the options for decorating the dress, Madame concludes: "... I know others, mothers several times over, who would be happy to be present at the triumph of a daughter, of a daughter-in-law, or perhaps — charming thought — a granddaughter. Which reminds us of a needful commonplace: that the shade ... must correspond to a person's age or looks; not to mention — something very commonly forgotten — that we have to reckon with the colour or shade of the wall hangings, that is to say with our background in any drawing room." Madame's

In past centuries, the quantity of fabric used in a dress was indicative of the wearer's wealth, and sometimes of social mood — hence slimmer silhouettes in the 1930s and 1940s, but more voluminous silhouettes in the 1950s and 1980s. Gianfranco Ferré's designs (opposite and right) are never stinting in their use of material.

From sketch to reality, the evolution of a couture gown, such as this one by Luca Luca, is a painstaking process, with many factors to consider. Most importantly, fabric choice must be appropriate to the design, able to drape, pleat, hold shape or cling as required.

❝*Anna was not in lilac, as Kitty had so urgently wished, but in a black, low-cut, velvet gown, showing her full throat and shoulders, that looked as though carved in old ivory, and her rounded arms, with tiny, slender wrists.*
Leo Tolstoy, *Anna Karenina*

The lines of the 1930s and 1940s inform two contemporary evening dresses: a strapless sheath by Martin Grant (left) which gives an overall impression of simplicity but is a masterwork of construction; and a bronze silk sheath with pleated and draped neckline (opposite) by Lisa Ho.

failsafe colours included silvery grey tulle, black tulle sewn over with jet, pastel mauve, yellow, twilight grey, "scabious" blue, emerald, and golden brown.

The "triumph of a daughter" referred to by Madame de Ponty was certainly one reason for attending a ball, but eventually this would necessitate its own event — the debutante ball, or "coming out". The origin of the debutante ball can be traced to the late eighteenth century when England's King George III and his wife Queen Charlotte introduced the idea to the court. The premise was that when a young woman reached marriageable age she would be presented to the royal family at a formal reception. The occasion would signify that a young woman was on the "market" for a husband, and with any luck she would be suitably matched with a mate before a year had passed.

In her book *Last Curtsey: The End of the Debutantes*, Fiona MacCarthy, notes that the ritual of "coming out" was once connected to the onset of menstruation. "Society doctors in the Victorian age advised the delay of a young girl's menstruation as long as possible, ideally until her formal 'coming out' at seventeen," she writes, "prescribing a strict regime of cold baths and exercise in the open air to allow her to make full use of the valuable formative years of puberty. The debutante would then emerge, butterfly from the chrysalis to parade before the eyes of her prospective suitors in 'the full perfection of womanhood.'"

Debutante dress was especially formal and adhered to a strict code for centuries. In Queen Victoria's time the expected attire was a long white court dress with ten-foot train, mystical white veil, ostrich feather headdress, elbow-length gloves.

Fiona MacCarthy recalls being one of the last debs to be presented to royalty before the practice was ended in 1958. By that time there was rather more diversity in dress choices, but not excessively so. As the author explains:

> In the contest for a suitable husband, ideally titled, landed and with money, originality had never been high on the agenda. Sameness and acceptability were of more value. In 1958 we looked alike in full-skirted calf-length dresses, long kid gloves and tiny hats constructed of myriad petals or soft feathers perched on our carefully waved hair. Whether the dresses had been made by a couturier, Victor Steibel and Norman Hartnell being the prestige names, or run up by the deb's mother's village dressmaker the final effect was curiously similar. I was wearing blue wild silk, the favoured fabric of that Season, and everywhere I looked were other girls in rustling skirts in the uniform light blue, turning Buckingham Palace to a shimmering silk sea. The Season was not just about the presentation, it encompassed

The neckpiece and mosaic beadwork of this silk chiffon dress by English designer Amanda Wakeley add a touch of exoticism and a modernist graphic sensibility to a supremely polished and elegant gown. Wakeley's designs typically adhere to a neutral palette and follow the natural shape of the body, reminiscent of classically inspired dress.

a series of lavish balls, country dances, cocktail parties and garden parties.

To be properly attired for the 1958 Season, a deb required numerous changes of clothing. According to Fiona MacCarthy: "A minimum of six dance dresses, of which one must be white for Queen Charlotte's Ball in May. Two or three of the dresses needed to be long and relatively formal, for the grander balls in London; the others could be short, for dances in the country."

Although the debutante presentation officially ended in 1958, its legacy continues. Debutante balls persist today in many countries, notably the US and Australia, and the choice of dress is almost always white, with white gloves. The history of the "coming out" is familiar to us from the novels of Jane Austen and her contemporaries, in which the highlight of a young woman's life was often the "coming out" Season. One of the most celebrated debutantes was the English aristocrat Lady Diana Manners.

Juliet Nicholson, in her book *The Perfect Summer*, vividly describes the dizzying whirl of parties that marked her coming out in 1911 at the age of eighteen:

> Lady Diana Manners was exhausted. On Thursday 1 June she emerged from her latest ball into the sunlight of a summer morning and was helped across the few steps from the door of Devonshire House in London's Park Lane to her carriage by the famous red-breasted, top-hatted "linkman" Mr Piddlecock, who gave her a cheery "Good Morning." As she was driven the short distance *en chaperone* with her mother from Devonshire House to her family's London home in Arlington Street off Piccadilly, she watched the dawn ritual of the streets being hosed down by men in rubber boots and rubber hats. She had been dancing for six hours in the white silk evening dress she had made herself, with coloured scarves wound turban-style around her curly hair. Her feet, tightly encased in pointy shoes, hurt as she stepped down from the carriage onto the cobblestones. Diana thought back on the relentless partying of the last two weeks, the first of her season as a debutante, and knew that with all the lunches, dinners, theatres and balls of the forthcoming month, she would be writing at least five "Collinses" a day. These thank you notes, requiring extensive consultation of a recognized dictionary in order to make them sufficiently original, accurate and ingratiating, took their nickname from the obsequious gratitude that flowed from the pen of Mr Collins in Jane Austen's novel, *Pride and Prejudice*. These letters were a great drain on time and imagination.

There is nothing more feminine than a pink dress. It conveys sweetness and gaiety. "Think Pink!" demanded Kay Gordon's fashion editor in the 1957 film Funny Face. *"Banish the black, burn the blue, and bury the beige," she declared. This fiction was not so far from reality; magazines of the day virtually dictated the "in" colours to their readers.*

Imagination and originality became a signature of the beautiful Lady Diana Manners, particularly in her dress. She was a trendsetter for her generation. Where other young debs might shop at one of the new department stores or employ a dressmaker to copy designs by the venerable French couturier Charles Frederick Worth, Lady Diana was more interested in the new styles being created in Paris by Paul Poiret.

Indeed, the turn of the century in England, as in much of the rest of Europe, marked a significant change in what women were wearing, not least of all to parties. According to Juliet Nicholson, "the fashions of the time positively invited flirtation and dalliance. For grander occasions women displayed erotically low-cut décolletage, and the innovative French couturier Paul Poiret had recently brought his sheer evening gown 'La Vague' across the Channel. The dress fell straight from the bosom to swirl seductively round the body, allowing a tantalising glimpse of the natural feminine curves beneath."

Although many women in England still slavishly followed the Paris fashions, there were also designers who moved away from the copying of mainstream styles, and in doing so shaped the fashion world themselves. In late nineteenth-century England, Lucy, Lady Duff Gordon became the top couturier of her day, influencing styles in England and beyond. Known by her design moniker, Lucile, Lady Duff Gordon began in earnest in the 1880s. "Lucy had started designing at a perfect time," write her biographers Meredith Etherington Smith and Jeremy Pilcher in *The It Girls*. "Rigid Victorian society was beginning to relax both its rules for entry and its behaviour. The old landed aristocracy was in the process of losing its power, and 'new money' was being let in, encouraged by the Prince of Wales. Rich Americans were coming to London to marry off their Dollar Princess daughters to Titles. The curtain was rising on the luxurious, lavish Edwardian era."

Indeed, the Edwardian era, which lasted from the beginning of the twentieth century to the outbreak of World War I, was a time of unprecedented partying. (A similar atmosphere reigned in France, although the Belle Époque truly began in the middle of the 1890s.) In England the new king, Edward, contributed to the mood of exuberant spending.

In *Edward VII and His Circle*, Virginia Cowles surmised that "Edwardian society modelled itself to suit the King's personal demands. Everything was larger than lifesize. There was an avalanche of balls and dinners and country house parties. More money was spent on clothes, more food was consumed, more horses were raced, more infidelities were committed, more birds were shot, more yachts were commissioned, more late hours were kept, than ever before."

The satin dress is a fashion classic, worn here by a young Carolina Herrera. In 1926 Dorothy Parker penned the lines: "Where's the man could ease a heart/Like a satin gown." Indeed satin became popular for eveningwear in the dance-crazy 1920s and 1930s, and in the disco era of the 1970s, because it looked and felt wonderful when the wearer moved.

Lucile was one of those who profited by the great demand for party dresses. As Meredith Etherington Smith and Jeremy Pilcher write: "Clothes were extremely important to these new society women; they were not grand enough to look dowdy, they had to be dressed to perfection. The smartly dressed woman could and did go to Paris to be dressed by Worth or by the new star, Jacques Doucet, if she was rich enough. But there was no guarantee that on her return to Mayfair, she would not see the same model on one of her friends. If she was not rich enough to go to Paris twice a year for clothes, then the society woman had to fall back on the needle of one of the 'little dressmakers' who abounded at that time and who were expert in copying the fashion plates in such publications as *Art, Goût, Beauté*. To have a tea-gown or morning dress or ball gown designed for her was a delightful idea indeed, and quickly caught on in a society ever hungry for novelty."

Lucile's business took off with a bang. One reason for her success was her striking colour palette, which included bold, brilliant combinations as well as the soft, pretty shades favoured by Edwardian ladies. And while her silhouettes essentially remained unchanged, she used exquisite decorative touches such as lace, braiding, sequins and handmade silk flowers to create intricate and beautifully feminine gowns. The other reason for her rapid rise to fame was the patronage of important women.

One early customer was Lady Angela Forbes, who recalled in later years: "I really think she did a great deal to revolutionise dress in London. All her frocks in those days even, were recognisable by her finishing touches, which generally consisted of minute buttons and little frills of lace and ribbon."

Society beauty and hostess Mrs Willie James, also reputedly mistress of Edward VII, was one of Lucile's most ardent clients. Mrs James was a fashion leader. According to Meredith Etherington Smith and Jeremy Pilcher, "A woman who wished to lead fashion in this era had to work extremely hard on choosing her clothes. The incredible variety of her wardrobe, with outfits designed for every occasion, was almost bewildering in its complexity."

The authors described a typical day thus: "On awakening in the morning, the fashionable woman opened her letters and drank her tea in bed dressed in a bewitching deshabillée dressing-gown. On coming downstairs, she would be dressed in a morning gown. If in London she would then pay calls in a walking dress or suit. If in the country, she would change into a tweed shooting suit to have lunch with the guns. At tea, when she received visitors in London, or took tea with the returned sportsmen in the country, she would wear a tea-gown. The final change was into la grande toilette for a dinner party; an even grander one for a ball, a visit to the opera or the theatre. A Saturday-to-Monday (as a weekend was then called in society) entailed no less than sixteen different changes,

Joanne Woodward dances with husband Paul Newman, while holding her Best Actress statuette for Three Faces of Eve, *at the 1958 Academy Awards party. Woodward wore a dress she had made herself, and later quipped that she was almost as proud of the dress as the award. Joan Crawford complained that the Oscar-winner had set Hollywood glamour back twenty years.*

In contrast to the strapless line, the plunging neckline is another variation of formal dress. In modern fashion terms its origin can be traced to the year 1913 when suddenly the V-neck was in and collars all but disappeared. The trend was denounced in churches as vulgar.

was often among them. After busy days of tennis, croquet and afternoon teas, the preparations began for the all-important evening events. Writes Juliet Nicholson in *The Perfect Summer*:

> On returning to the cool of the house the ladies consulted Mrs Eric Pritchard's excellent guide to fashions *The Cult of Chiffon* and retired to their bedrooms to change into floaty tea-gowns — because, as Mrs Pritchard advised, "when the tea urn sings at five o'clock we can don these garments of poetical beauty." After tea — ginger biscuits especially brought in from Biarritz (they had been Edward VII's favourite), scones, egg sandwiches and three sorts of cake (including chocolate) — a rubber of bridge, with a plate of nourishing "bridge rolls" on the side-table, relieved the tedium before it was time for the ladies to change into something described by Diana as a "little less limp".

accompanied by hats, gloves, blouses, corsets, shoes, furs, evening cloaks and jewels. Three or four domed trunks were not an unusual accompaniment when such a fashionable woman went to a house party."

Belvoir Castle in Leicestershire, principal country seat of the aristocratic Rutland family, was the setting for many a glamorous house party. Almost every Saturday-to-Monday through the summer season, rich and well-connected visitors arrived from London. Young society beauty Lady Diana Manners

It is no wonder that corsets were required for the next change, into formal dress for dinner. The women needed at least an hour for their beauty routine. The skin was whitened with creams and white rice powder, and then blue crayon used to highlight the veins at the neck, temple and cleavage. Eyebrows and eyelashes were darkened using elderflower berries or

Bold, brash and sometimes in dubious taste, the 1980s party dress conveyed a sense of great confidence using dramatic decorative devices, such as the shoulder bow, as in Carolina Herrera's black and white creation (left), and jewel colours, evident in Bill Blass' designs (opposite).

a cork that had been singed in the flame of a candle. According to Juliet Nicholson, the final stages of the grand toilette involved clamping small silver rings into the nipples to deepen and raise the cleavage "by providing a sort of ledge on which the evening gown rested precariously." The author sets the scene for the evening, describing the ostentation of the country house formal dinner: "The dining table would be decorated with orchids and cyclamen, and after an eight-course dinner at a grand house like Belvoir, eaten off Charles II silver and Charles II gold, the ladies would leave the gentlemen for a period … Later there might be more bridge in the study, or an amusing session of charade in the gardenia and stephanotis-scented drawing room. A large dish of crystallised violets often sat on the piano in case an impromptu player or his accompanying singer should suddenly feel peckish."

At other English country houses the occasion would be grander still. At Renishaw in Derbyshire, there was a full orchestra transported from London. At nearby Chatsworth, the guests might stage their own play in the estate's private theatre.

Just as in past eras the formal party had provided an opportunity for young women to meet a suitable mate, the country house parties of the Edwardian era provided many opportunities for flirtatious encounters, and more. As Juliet Nicholson writes

of those Saturday-to-Monday parties: "During the day, a clandestine affair could develop unobserved while family portraits were being admired in the picture gallery, or in a dark corner of the library, or out walking in magnificent gardens … At night, the names written on cards slotted into brass holders on the bedroom doors were as helpful to lovers as to the maids bringing early morning tea … At six in the morning a hand-bell rung on each of the bedroom floors gave guests time to return to their own beds before the early morning tea trays arrived."

The fin-de-siecle, in both England and France as well as other centres of wealth and fashion such as Vienna, represented a great age for formal dress. The sense of luxury imbued in fashions was unrivalled by anything that had come before in that century or that followed. For evening clothes, favoured fabrics were crepe de chine, chiffon, mousseline de soie, tulle and satin, the latter embroidered with floral patterns, adorned with ribbons or painted by hand. Fashion historian James Laver notes in his book *Costume and Fashion*, that "the amount of sheer labour which went into the making of one fashionable gown was truly prodigious; one would have to go back to the embroidered brocades of the early eighteenth century to find anything comparable."

However, as the dawn of the twentieth-century approached there also began to be a change in

At various times in fashion history, the classical robes of Greece and Rome have provided a source of inspiration for evening dress. Aside from the ubiquitous toga party, at which guests dress up in the guise of ancient Romans, there have been many more sophisticated takes on the simple draped robe, such as this Bill Blass design from 1989.

The 1980s saw trends changing at a mercurial rate. In America, the dominant look was rich, elegant and feminine, which in many ways reflected the taste of First Lady, Nancy Reagan. Two designs from Bill Blass typify the era, from 1980 (left) and 1984 (opposite).

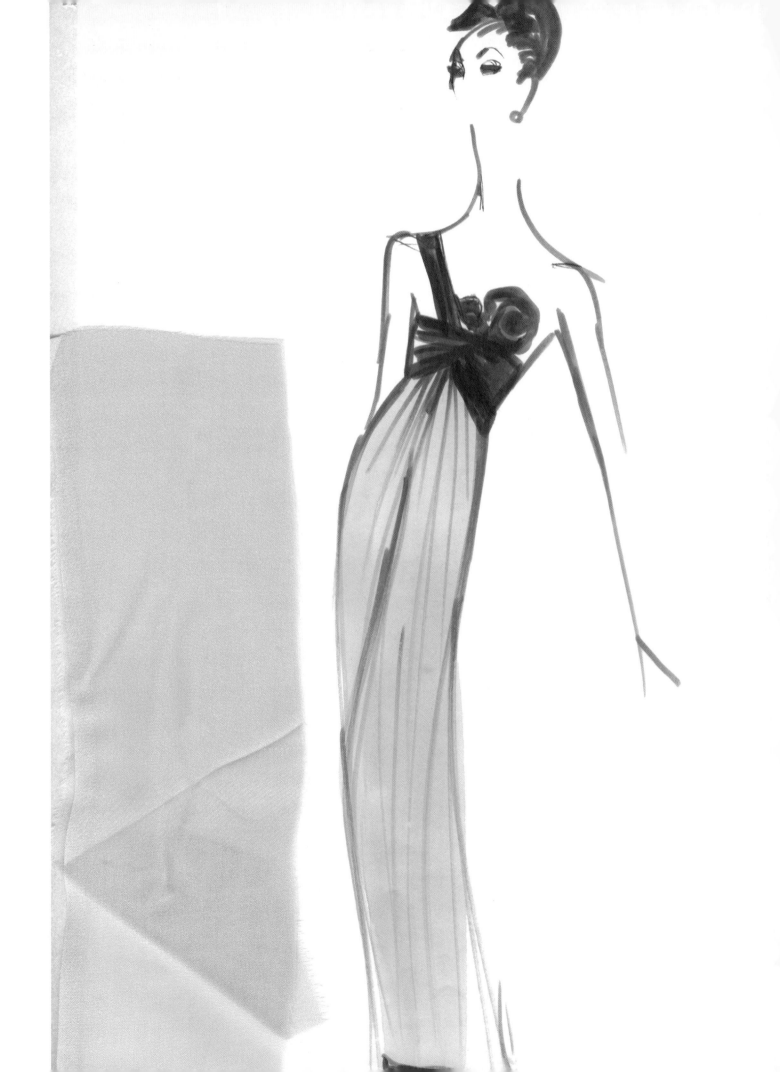

women's dress. Sport was having a profound effect not only on day clothes but evening clothes as well. Women wanted to move and have freedom to dance some of the new, energetic, jazz-inspired steps. Simultaneously, the idea of going out to public places for an evening's entertainment took hold. A distinct era in dress was about to open, with new ways of dressing for evening, and new types of partying.

Even so, the appeal of formal dressing did not really dwindle in the early decades of the twentieth century; it simply adapted to the times. The occasions for wearing a long formal dress were certainly not as prevalent as they had been, but in some respects this only made the formal gown all the more precious.

In his novel of 1929, *The Party Dress*, American author Joseph Hergesheimer builds a story around the character of American housewife Nina Henry, who at the age of forty-two, orders her first evening gown from Paris. Getting ready for the party that will change the course of her life, Nina, standing in front of the mirror, "had had an amazing glimpse of herself in the black dress Ishtarre had made in Paris … a tightly fitted satin bodice caught in points on each shoulder and a very full tulle skirt, not so short as it might have been, with a dip at the left side. That is how Nina Henry would have described it, but her words would have meant nothing. It meant nothing at all to speak of the dress as a dress. An affair of satin and tulle. It was like the effect of magic — Nina scarcely recognised herself."

The transforming effect of the evening dress is a phenomenon that reached its apex, at least in modern times, in the middle of the twentieth century. In the 1950s the Paris dress became the *dernier cri* in formal elegance, especially if it came from the House of Dior. "All the girls dreamed of wearing Dior," recalled *Vogue* magazine's Edmonde Charles-Roux, who was persuaded to buy a floor-length crinoline gown on sale, despite the fact that it weighed about twenty-seven kilos, or sixty pounds, and therefore she could barely dance a step when wearing it.

The ultra-feminine New Look gown, with its tiny wasp waist and billowing skirt was made for the red carpet. One of Dior's most devoted Hollywood clients was Olivia de Havilland who estimated she had bought two hundred of his dresses over the years. Elizabeth Taylor, too, was a regular visitor to the Paris salon.

Balenciaga, Givenchy and Jacques Fath also developed a devoted following among the high-profile stars of the silver screen, and the costume designers at the major studios were quick to interpret the Paris trends in their outfits for both film and public appearances. At the 1955 Academy Awards, Best Actress winner Grace Kelly memorably wore an ice blue gown by Paramount costume designer Edith Head.

In the 1990s women rejected the luxurious exhibitionism of dress in the previous decade, and opted for an understated, more sober style that often verged on the minimal. Master of the look is Giorgio Armani, whose perfect cutting, elegant purity and neutral colour palette represented the new informal approach to party dressing.

Before the industrial age, gold clothing was not only prohibitively expensive, as it contained real gold, but the law often controlled who could wear it. An English proclamation of 1559 stipulated: "None shall wear in his apparel any cloth of gold, silver, or tinsel; satin, silk, or cloth mixed with gold or silver, nor any sables; except earls and all of superior degrees." A modern example of the gold dress by Jayson Brundson (opposite) and a beaded sheath from 1958 by Helen Rose (above).

The clean straight line of the strapless bodice allows for an almost infinite variety of decorative effects, including the rigid horizontal pleating on Balmain's 1950s gown (previous page, left); a delicate fringed ruffle on the party dress worn by Leslie Caron, pictured with Shirley MacLaine in 1955 (previous page, right); filigree lace in black on Carven's white creation (above) and the wrapped effect of Giorgio Armani's vermilion showstopper (opposite).

The Oscars remain one of the year's most watched formal occasions, enjoyed vicariously by millions of viewers with one thing in mind: who's wearing what. In his afterword to David Friend's book, *Oscar Night*, journalist Dominick Dunne recalls the Vanity Fair party at which he was seated on the same table as Elizabeth Taylor and Audrey Hepburn.

"I knew them both," he writes, "but I was always stunned by their magnificence. Just watching those two legends cry out each other's name and lean across the table to kiss-kiss made the evening an event. Audrey was one of the best-dressed women in the world, the height of understated style, and that night she had on a black evening dress by Givenchy. Elizabeth was bedecked in a huge diamond necklace and a huge diamond ring. 'Kenny Lane?' asked Audrey, pointing at the necklace. 'No, Mike Todd,' answered Elizabeth, mentioning her third husband. 'Kenny Lane?' asked Audrey, indicating the ring. 'No, Richard Burton,' replied Elizabeth, mentioning her fifth and sixth husband. With that the two stars screamed with laughter and kissed again."

It seems that despite the revolutionary changes in the lives of women over the last five hundred years, the passion for lavish party dresses remains undimmed. Even if not all of us have the opportunity to wear such fabulous creations we certainly love to see, and critique, the public figures wearing them. Few would argue with Dominick Dunne when he summarises the irresistible allure of that most glittering of formal occasions, the Academy Awards.

"Oscar night is *the* party night in Hollywood — New Year's Eve and the Fourth of July rolled into one — and since 1994 the *Vanity Fair* party has been the one to be seen at," writes Dunne, who attended his first Oscar party in 1955, at Romanoff's. He maintains that because the *Vanity Fair* party is so hard to get into, it makes it all the more desirable. "Such glamour, such swank, such high fashion, and, above all, such star power," he enthuses. "The crowd outside cheers the famous descending from their limousines, and the journalists, lined up behind velvet ropes, scream the stars' names, take flash photos, and hold out microphones. You enter on a high at five in the afternoon, and the high lasts until three or four o'clock in the morning. For someone like me, who loves to mingle with movie stars, it's Nirvana. *Hi, Nicole. Hi, Sean. Hi, Renée. Hi, Anjelica. Oh, my God, there's Charlize Theron, carrying her Oscar! Introduce me.*"

The Far Eastern influence on fashion has been considerable. It began with the craze for Chinoiserie in the eighteenth century, developed with Japonisme in the second half of of the nineteenth century, and continues to impact on the styles, fabrics and colours used by contemporary designers. Giorgio Armani's daring dress with cut-out bodice and patterned silk skirt clearly takes its cue from the motif on a Chinese lacquerwork cabinet inlaid with mother of pearl.

Historically, colourful dress has been the preserve of the aristocracy. During the first half of the sixteenth century the upper classes of Central and Northern Europe wore extremely bright hues – red was a particular favourite – until the fashions of Spain made black and sombre tones more popular. Four designs by Escada ran the gamut from vivid to monochrome, while the purity of black and white informs the elegant eveningwear of Carmen Marc Valvo (overleaf).

〜 *One of the signatures of a formal dress is embellished fabric, as in Grimaldi Giardina's beaded gown (above) and Lorenzo Riva's design in metallic lace (opposite). The idea dates to late Medieval and Renaissance times when the very rich wore material woven with real gold or silver and stitched precious jewels onto their finest clothes to signify their wealth.*

Black remains the "safe" choice for formal wear, but can be far from conservative, as these styles by Georges Chakra attest. Prior to Chanel's "little black dress" of the 1920s, the black dress had enjoyed unprecedented popularity during the reign of Queen Victoria, who continued to wear the colour of mourning long after her husband's death.

Chapter Three

The Cocktail Party

"Something about glamour interested me. All my schoolbooks had drawings of women on terraces with a cocktail and a cigarette."

Bill Blass, from his memoir Bare Blass

The very phrase "cocktail party" brings to mind a specific place and point in time — New York in the 1950s and 1960s, when society embraced more relaxed modes of entertaining, and when the idea of the early evening drink gathered momentum as an event worth celebrating. Where hosting a formal do required plenty of money and a grand venue, almost anyone with a bit of imagination and a well-stocked liquor cabinet could throw a cocktail party. Fun rather than formality was the watchword. After World War II, fashions had changed to accompany the new lifestyles taking shape in America. A mood of youthful optimism reigned, and women embraced it with gusto. Apart from the sportier look of her day clothes, the fashionable woman also added a crucial item to her wardrobe, the cocktail dress.

Writing in 1964, French style guru Genevieve Antoine Dariaux noted that although women might wear suits and separates during the day, from 6pm, she advised, "the dress comes into its own again, in the form of a cocktail or dinner dress. This is the moment of triumph for the famous little black dress, somewhat décolleté, made of sheer wool or silk crepe, and with all of its chic concentrated in its cut and line." More specifically, "the perfect hostess wears a dress that is only slightly décolleté, or not

Although the 1950s are typically associated with the little black cocktail dress, vivid hues were also very popular for party wear. In 1952 the Paris shows were full of brilliant colours: reds, pinks, oranges and greens, and feminine floral themes proliferated. This rose-pink dress, photographed by Cecil Beaton, is typical of the period.

at all, but a rich material. If she has a good figure she may even wear a very simple full-length soft wool sheath with a high neckline."

The look is immortalised in the 1961 film of Truman Capote's novella *Breakfast at Tiffany's*. Audrey Hepburn portrays the character of Holly Golightly whose life seems to be an endless whirl of cocktail parties, and whose wardrobe seems to comprise a fabulous array of little Givenchy dresses, all accessorised with neat purses, stoles, hats and costume jewellery. Nearly every morning she is to be found at the door of her apartment block — still in chic cocktail attire from the party the night before — buzzing upstairs neighbour Mr Yunioshi to let her in as she has forgotten her keys. By day, Golightly's wardrobe appears to consist of little more than a sleep mask, a man's shirt or a trench coat. Otherwise it is almost always cocktail hour in her world.

The iconic dress of the film is a slim black Givenchy number worn by Audrey Hepburn in the opening scene of the film. In the book, *Audreystyle*, Pamela Clark Keogh describes it thus: "It's 6am on Fifth Avenue — and Audrey Hepburn is down on her luck as Holly Golightly; she's got a case of the mean reds that only a visit to Tiffany's can cure. Holding coffee in a paper cup and nibbling a Danish, Miss Golightly envisions brighter days. The first thing that strikes us is her beauty. She has secrets, she is kind, she is worldly, she dreams of love. Dressed in a black dress, slim as a line, her upper arms lithe and yearning, wearing paste jewellery as she contemplates the real thing, she looks in at a world more peaceful, more ordered, more glittering than her own — having breakfast at Tiffany's."

The black cocktail dress, Audrey style — sleeveless, high-necked with simple straight lines, and unadorned save for costume jewellery and accessories — became an instant fashion classic whether short or long. Both versions were made by Givenchy for *Breakfast at Tiffany's*, long for the opening scene and short for the film stills. When the dress worn by Hepburn in the film was auctioned for charity by Christie's in London at the end of 2006 it fetched a record price for popular cultural memorabilia. The winning anonymous phone bid was for 410,000 pounds sterling. There was much speculation over who had secured the dress. Victoria Beckham was initially thought to have made the purchase, until it was revealed that the house of Givenchy had bought the dress for its archives.

Reporting on the sale, British newspaper *The Independent* commented, "That's a lot of money for a sleeveless sheath but perhaps it's reasonable for a garment the magazine *Harper's Bazaar* recently hailed as 'one of the great fashion moments in cinema history'. The dress, designed by Hubert de

In 1950 a new line, the sheath, replaced the New Look. It hugged the body and emphasised a shapely silhouette. The same year saw a new passion for chiffon, evident in this cocktail dress with matching coat by Cristobal Balenciaga. The dress is made from hundreds of scalloped bands of silk chiffon sewn on a straight slip.

Givenchy, gave Hepburn an enduring status as a style icon — and gave millions of women a solution to the vexing question of what to wear whenever they've nothing to wear."

In fact the popularity of the little black party dress, like cocktail culture itself, predates *Breakfast at Tiffany's* by several decades. To properly understand the origins of cocktail fashions and the cocktail party it is important to understand the culture of the cocktail drink.

Debrett's Etiquette and Modern Manners takes pains to differentiate between the cocktail itself and the cocktail party: "While the cocktail (a mixture of spirits and other ingredients) is not often served nowadays, it has given its name to the type of party that starts at 6pm or 6.30pm and continues for about two hours. Guests may be offered sherry only, champagne only, red and white wine, a wine cup or a variety of spirits and aperitifs. At least one non-alcoholic drink must also be provided. Food is light, and is presented in such a way that it can be eaten easily with the fingers." Although it might seem somewhat pointless to make the distinction, in fact the idea of the cocktail party emerged at least a century after the birth of the drink from which it takes its name. And the cocktail party, at which cocktails or alcoholic drinks are consumed in

a private arena, helped to make drinking acceptable for women. One of the first published references to the cocktail drink comes from an 1806 edition of a New York weekly, *The Balance*, which stated that a "cocktail is a stimulating liquor composed of spirits of any kind, sugar, water, bitters …"

Alcoholic drinks had been mixed since medieval times, when ale was combined with mead to create a drink known as a Bragget. In Britain, the Victorians

The little black dress has become a staple of cocktail attire and can be sleeveless and décolleté, or cover the arms and throat. Slim Aarons' photograph of Audrey Hepburn at a party in 1953 (opposite) captures the elegance of mid-century cocktail style. Jean Yu's sweet dress with soft balloon skirt (right) is a modern interpretation.

drank cocktails with imaginative names such as the Gum Tickler and Corpse Reviver, which supposedly brought health benefits. Across the Atlantic, in the state of Virginia, mint sprigs were added to rum or brandy and served as morning pick-me-ups in the eighteenth century. This drink became known as the Mint Julep.

The most famous of modern cocktails, the martini, is said to have originated in the 1860s, when a San Francisco bartender, Jerry Thomas, concocted a drink for a gold miner on his way to the town of Martinez. Thomas accordingly dubbed the drink "The Martinez" and included it in his bartender's guide book, listing the ingredients as Old Tom gin, sweet vermouth, a dash of maraschino and bitters, a slice of lemon and two dashes of gum syrup. Another piece of cocktail lore ties the name martini to the Martini-Henry rifle used by the British army in the late nineteenth century, purportedly because both rifle and drink had a strong kick.

Whatever its origins, it seems clear that the purpose of the cocktail was to stimulate and enliven, and by the end of the nineteenth century it was starting to become a very popular drink. The martini was one of the first drinks on the barman's menu and the list steadily grew to embrace a staggering number of ingredients and combinations. By 1900 the martini was also being consumed in London's fashionable bars and clubs.

The cocktail shaker was an integral part of the drink-making process, and turned the task of cocktail making into a form of entertainment. Part of the fun of ordering a cocktail was, and still is, watching the barman mix it.

In his book, *Vintage Bar Ware*, Stephen Visakay maintains that by the late 1800s the bartender's shaker as we know it today had become a standard tool of the trade. "At the turn of the century, New

The black cocktail dress originated in the 1920s. It was considered modern and chic, yet it also suited the egalitarian mood that held sway after World War I. Even the couturier Worth declared in 1921 that "simplicity is praiseworthy and suited to our present conditions of life." That did not mean luxury was banished: Jeanne Lanvin's embellished dress (above), for example, or the tiered silk chiffon designs worn by Lee Miller and Marion Moreshouse Cummings (opposite).

York City hotels were serving the English custom of five o'clock tea and it was a short leap to the five o'clock cocktail hour …"

Although the proliferation of bars and drinking establishments certainly encouraged cocktail consumption, such places were not deemed acceptable for most women. However, the home *was* seen as an appropriate setting for cocktail mixing and imbibing, and enabled women in general to also participate. As early as 1899, a novel by Kate Chopin, *The Awakening*, included a scene in which the protagonist Edna Pontellier mixes and serves a cocktail at a grand dinner she is hosting. Once everyone is seated, but before the dinner begins, Edna presents the cocktail, the colour of a garnet and poured into tiny glasses. One of the guests, Miss Mayblunt, "begged to be allowed to keep her cocktail untouched before her, just to look at. The colour was marvellous. She could compare it with nothing she had ever seen …"

Several years later in 1906, Isabella Beeton included a section on cocktails (one of which was The Manhattan) in her *Mrs Beeton's Book of Household Management*. The following year Rachel Crothers' play, *The Coming of Mrs Patrick*, contained a scene in which Mrs Patrick makes a cocktail at home, "rushing to the sideboard and pouring something

The contemporary cocktail dress code allows the wearer to freely accessorise (opposite), but between the 1930s and 1960s matching a dress with shoes, a cocktail hat and gloves was considered de rigueur (right).

Throughout the twentieth century, fashions for the cocktail party continued to evolve and now include many styles, from simple black shifts to beautiful concoctions wrought in sequins, feathers and paillettes. Anna Molinari's designs (left) run the gamut from fun and flirty to gowns more suited to a formal occasion. Vintage gold cocktail dress by Nina Ricci (overleaf, left) and beaded extravaganza by Gianfranco Ferre (overleaf, right).

The dress must not hang on the body but follow its lines. It must accompany its wearer and when a woman smiles the dress must smile with her.
Madeleine Vionnet

of everything into the glass," according to the stage directions. One of the characters in Edith Wharton's 1907 novel *The Fruit of the Tree*, Mrs Carbury, is described as "leaving everywhere in her wake a trail of cigarette ashes and cocktail glasses."

While novelty could account to some extent for the growing popularity of the cocktail in America, there was a whole raft of social and political changes that made cocktail drinking very much a part of popular culture. Francis W. Crowninshield, an arbiter of manners and style and the first editor of *Vanity Fair*, was compelled to write in 1909 that "The telephone, coeducation, wireless telegraphy, motor cars, millionaires, bridge whist, women's rights, Sherry's, cocktails, four-day liners, pianolas, steam heat, directoire gowns, dirigible ball gowns, and talking machines have all contributed to an astonishing social metamorphosis."

In particular the youth of America began to break away from long-held traditions and a sense of familial duty to embrace the concepts of independence, leisure, consumerism and freedom of movement — thanks firstly to the bicycle and secondly to the automobile. Instead of spending evenings and weekends with family at home, the young people of America went out. Girls especially enjoyed a newfound liberation and openly flaunted conventions of appropriate

A small sleeve and simple scoop neck add a sense of decorum to the cocktail dress. Nineteen-year-old Brigitte Bardot still smoulders in her demure dress (opposite) accompanied by husband film director Roger Vadim at the 1955 Cannes Film Festival. A modern take on the covered style by Luca Luca (right) employs a shorter hemline.

behaviour and dress. They fuelled the explosion in nightlife and nightclubs, and popularised public drinking for women.

In his book *Flapper*, Joshua Zeitz chronicles the case of nineteen-year-old New York heiress Eugenia Kelly who in 1915 was brought before the Yorkville Magistrate to answer charges of wayward behaviour. The public eagerly followed the case, captivated not only by the fact that it was Eugenia's own mother who had sworn out the arrest warrant, but that the young woman seemed to embody the fears of countless American parents over their daughters' behaviour.

"Eugenia, it seemed, had turned overnight from a sweet young society belle into an irredeemable wild child … For months Eugenia had been frequenting the dance halls on Broadway, where she acquired an insatiable appetite for jazz, cigarettes and brandy," writes Zeitz. She had also taken up with an older man and threatened to elope with him. However, when her mother threatened to cut off her inheritance, Eugenia eventually agreed to toe the line and do as her mother said, although the good behaviour didn't last for long. But, as Zeitz, comments, "The guardians of feminine virtue and Victorian morality had much bigger problems with which to contend. Every girl, it seemed, wanted to be Eugenia Kelly. It was the age of the flapper."

 Diana Vreeland once declared, "I adore pink. I love the pale Persian pinks of the little carnations of Provence, and Schiaparelli's pink, the pink of the Incas. And, though it's so vieux jeu *I can hardly bear to repeat it, pink is the navy blue of India." Cerise dress here by J Mendel.*

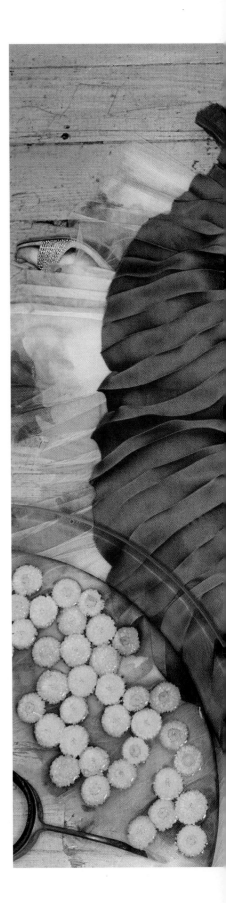

The silhouette of the cocktail dress has varied wildly over the past century, from the fitted frock with defined waist (left) — this example by Martin Grant — to the voluminous cocoon — exemplified by Givenchy (opposite) — which reveals little of the body underneath.

Newspapers and magazines reported on the flapper phenomenon almost daily. And from the start she was associated with cocktails, among other vices. The US secretary of labor referred to the "flippancy of the cigarette-smoking, cocktail-drinking flapper." *New Republic* editor Bruce Bliven wrote a profile of a flapper, whom he dubbed "Jane", whose "minister, poor man" condemned her as "a perfectly horrible example of wild youth — paint, cigarettes, cocktail, petting parties — ooh!"

One of America's most famous flappers was Zelda Fitzgerald, who together with her husband, author F. Scott Fitzgerald, embodied the spirit of the times. In the words of silent screen star Lillian Gish, "they didn't *make* the twenties; they *were* the twenties." The couple's ability to party became legendary. Joshua Zeitz calls them the most celebrated couple of the Jazz Age, "metaphorically drunk on Scott's success, and quite literally intoxicated by the steady stream of champagne and gin that they began pouring into their systems." They didn't crave formal entertainments; anywhere they could get a drink was a potential venue for a party. Zeitz reports that "When, after several days they were evicted from the Biltmore Hotel for causing too much noise and too much damage, Scott and Zelda moved their Honeymoon to the Commodore. They celebrated the change in itinerary by spinning around in the hotel's revolving door for more than half an hour and passing several delirious weeks drinking, attending rooftop parties, frequenting the theatre, and generally burning through Scott's magazine royalties faster than they came in."

Black lace became fashionable in the eighteenth century, with most of the production centred in Chantilly, France. Like white lace it was considered as valuable as fine jewellery. Even in an age of industry, we still think of it as reserved for special garments such as these cocktail dresses by Grimaldi Giardina (opposite) and Bill Blass (below).

The Fitzgeralds loved publicity, and the nature of the drinks party, of which they might attend several in one evening, gave them the perfect opportunity for spontaneous acts and came with none of the restrictions of a more formal "do". After all, if the purpose of a party was to consume cocktails, or any type of alcohol, then there was no need to hold back. Being outrageous was par for the course.

Joshua Zeitz describes how the Fitzgeralds crisscrossed America for three years. "At every destination, they brought chaos and excitement with them and left behind a trail of broken bottles and fantastic stories." It was not unusual for the couple to arrive at parties, with Scott perched on the bonnet of the taxicab and Zelda cheering from the roof. In a typically eccentric display, Zelda took to disrobing at parties and taking long hot baths.

If Zelda was America's first flapper, then Lois Long must surely take the honours for runner-up. She was the archetypal Jazz Age girl, out all night, and penning witty columns for *The New Yorker* by day. Writing under the pseudonym "Lipstick", Long famously chronicled the parties and nightlife of Manhattan. The influential columnist was one of the city's most dynamic women, both gorgeous and outrageous. She truly lived the life of the party-hopping flapper. At *The New Yorker* offices it was not unusual for Long to come into work at three or four in the morning.

"Fresh from a night on the town, dressed to the nines, and flush from hours of heavy drinking," writes Joshua Zeitz, "Long managed consistently to leave the key to her enclosed cubicle at home and amused her colleagues by kicking off her heels, climbing in stocking feet onto the doorknob of her workstation, and hoisting herself over the partition wall. In hot weather she'd casually strip down to her slip and clack away at her typewriter."

For a drinking woman like Long, and any flapper worth her salt in America, Prohibition, which had been introduced in 1920, merely added a frisson of excitement to nightly revels on the town. It certainly did nothing to deter drinking, and may have had the opposite effect. Champagne producers in France, for example, found that sales of their bubbly in the United States tripled in the years of Prohibition, despite the challenges of smuggling their product into the country.

During Prohibition even the more conservative sections of society were caught up in the cocktail craze. In his book *Drink*, Andrew Barr maintains that "Cocktails became all the rage among young people in the early 1920s because they were regarded as new and American, and because by drinking cocktails they were able to outrage their elders." However it was probably not the cocktail itself that provoked outrage; more the quantity and quality of alcohol

French actress Jeanne Moreau, in a white Chanel dress, epitomises mid-century cocktail glamour at the 13th International Cannes Film Festival held in 1960. She is accompanied by Jean-Paul Belmondo, her co-star in the Peter Brook's film Moderato Cantibile. *Moreau won the Best Actress award for her role.*

❦⁓ *Yves Saint Laurent was adept at combining the structured elements of couture with an impression of airiness and freedom. His "L'Eléphant Blanc" haute couture dress (opposite) for the spring/summer 1958 collection of Christian Dior is a case in point. Designer Martin Grant's sketches for his collection (above) range from slim, straight lines to bubble hems and balloon sleeves.*

consumed that gave rise to parental consternation. In any event, by the end of the 1920s the cocktail had become well and truly popularised.

Prohibition certainly did nothing to dampen the enthusiasm of Lois Long, the Lipstick columnist, for alcohol. As Joshua Zeitz explains, "Long used her column to flaunt the drinking habits and adventures of young women like herself who no longer felt bound by Victorian notions of feminine propriety. What reader could forget the week she stayed out until dawn, realised that her copy was due at *The New Yorker* by noon, rushed to the office still decked out in a backless evening dress, threw up a few times in the bathroom, and still managed to bang out her column before the deadline?"

"I shall not write about restaurants," she wrote in one column, "because I haven't been to any and I am tired about writing about eating anyway. I shall write about drinking, because it is high time that somebody approached the subject in a specific, constructive way." Given her penchant for liquor, it was no surprise when New York socialite Barney Gallant invented a new cocktail, The Lipstick, naming it after the glamourous columnist. It comprised two parts champagne, one part gin, one part orange juice, a dash of grapefruit juice, and a trickle of cherry brandy. "Sweet but with a wallop," went the accompanying description.

Lois Long, like other flappers, was not so interested in food and certainly not in cooking it, and in embracing the solo consumption of alcohol (without food being essential) set in motion a new set of ideas about 'drinks' as reason enough for a party, an idea that would be picked up with relish by the rest of society in the following decade. For now, though, nights out drinking and drinks parties were rather the preserve of the flapper and her man.

The flapper not only wanted to live the high life; she also wanted to look the part while doing so, and flapper style did not come cheap, at least in the early days, as more varied outfits became required for the flapper's dizzy social life. For the working week, she needed ensembles that would be practical enough for getting around town and performing work tasks in, but stylish enough to suit a modern, fashion-conscious woman. For weekends she needed sporty outfits for daytime wear, and for almost any night of the week she needed evening dresses that were elegant yet informal enough for speakeasies and nightclubs, and, in shape at least, allowed for vigorous dance steps such as The Charleston. Thus the 1920s marked not only a pivotal turning point in fashions in general, but in particular they gave rise to the idea of dressing for cocktails.

According to Glynis Ward in her essay "Cocktail Wear", social drinking tended to be done undercover

As cocktail parties usually involve many people crowded into a single venue, the hats worn by women at such events had to be kept small and close to the head, so as not to be obstructive. For the same reason, the overall cocktail ensemble was purposefully slimline, with detail at the neckline and framing the face, best suited for viewing close up.

Cocktail dresses are often tied with a bow, whether below the bust or at the natural waistline: Photographer John Swope, a close friend of Henry Fonda, sits with actress Jane Fonda during a cocktail party given for her in August 1959 (above). Red dress by Bill Blass 1961 (opposite).

Combining elements of tuxedo styling and the crisp detailing of a band-leader's uniform with its ribbon edging and rows of tiny buttons, Alice McCall's black and white dress reveals the legs but covers the rest of the body.

❧ Black and white are still the most popular choices for cocktail wear: combined together, as in Reem Acra's patterned strapless dress (above); all-white with matching gloves by Bill Blass (overleaf, left); or dramatic ebony from top to toe by Givenchy (overleaf, right).

during Prohibition, either at home or in speakeasies. A cocktail party — provided you could find the alcohol — was easy to organise, and there were always plenty of available guests. As cocktail parties were much less formal than dinner parties or balls, a new type of clothing was needed — something less ornate than an evening gown yet more adorned than day wear. "The first cocktail dresses surfaced during the mid-1920s," notes Glynis Ward, "and were similar to the waistless, loose cut of the flapper dress. Indeed, most of the women who wore cocktail dresses were flappers. Originally designed for the young, the dresses barely grazed the knee. Many dresses were heavily beaded or had fringes; typical fabrics were silk and layered chiffon." The flapper's drop-waisted styles have come and gone in fashion since, but the premise of the shorter hem for cocktail dresses has remained firmly in place.

The other enduring legacy of the 1920s cocktail era is the all-important accessory. Glynis Ward notes that "cocktail clothing was accompanied by specialised accessories. Tiny bags, just big enough for money and powder were encrusted in sequins and rhinestones, set in a frame, most often with a small chain handle. Shoes were slipper-like, and often dyed to match dress or purse. Elbow length or shorter gloves and small hat were worn by guests, but the hostess remained more casual, without hat, purse or gloves. These accessories became traditional to cocktail dressing, and remained as part of the fashion through the mid-60s."

Lois Long recommended accessories of a different kind to any girl worthy of the name flapper. "As an

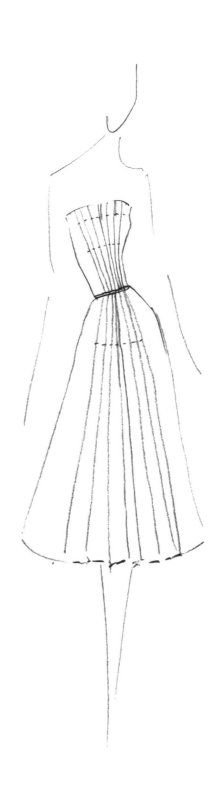

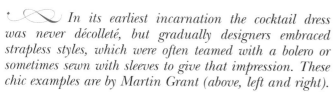 *In its earliest incarnation the cocktail dress was never décolleté, but gradually designers embraced strapless styles, which were often teamed with a bolero or sometimes sewn with sleeves to give that impression. These chic examples are by Martin Grant (above, left and right).*

accompaniment to grown-up sport of any kind," she recommended "a quart cocktail shaker, four glasses, a bottle opener and corkscrew, strainer and squeezer, all fitting into a suede bag four-and-a-half inches by three inches in size."

Elyssa Da Cruz, writing for The Costume Institute at The Metropolitan Museum of Art, makes the point that aside from the twenties era bringing the cocktail dress to life, cocktail wear, with its all-important accessories, actually became a signature look of the decade. She explains that:

> By 1929, with the aid of liberation parties like the Women's Organization for National Prohibition Reform, women had become more visible in the social sphere and the "modern woman" was born. This "Drinking Woman" was an ideal rooted in newfound concepts of individuality and a denial of Edwardian matronly functions. She emerged at private cocktail soirées and lounges, and the cocktail dress, as a short evening sheath with matching hat, shoes, and gloves, was designated to accompany her … Cocktail garb, by virtue of its flexibility and functionality, became the 1920s uniform for the progressive fashionable elite.

From the mid-1950s onwards women demanded youthful party dresses, with knee-length hems and charming details. Recent examples include tuxedo styling on a strapless sheath (previous page, left), an abundance of frills and ruffles (previous page, right), oversized sleeves (left) and a bodice of tiny beaded flowers (right).

It is true that the first few years of the twentieth century saw the emergence of a new type of social culture that centred much more around public life than it did on private life. Where women of the Edwardian era or fin de siecle, strove for feminine perfection in their attire and behaviour, the twentieth-century woman was all about modernity. And although the idea of the drinking woman, wearing cocktail attire that was specially designated for her purposes, seemed a complete turnaround from the matronly Edwardian era, it did in fact have its roots in an Edwardian fashion leader, the demimondaine.

In *The Elegant Woman*, Gertrude Aretz, describes the emergence of the new woman of fashion: "About 1900 the rise of the American bar and the nightclub to the level of social institutions brought with it an entirely new type of demimondaine. Elegant, cultured women began to be seen every evening at exclusive and luxurious night haunts run for the entertainment of rich men of Society ... Their education, as a rule was good. They professed a cosmopolitan culture, spoke several languages, or at least English and French, and had a superficial knowledge of literature and art. They had visited every fashionable pleasure resort in Europe, and were accomplished women of the world ... They never committed a faux pas, and in their dress showed a perfect taste which was envied by real ladies. Their breeding was perfect, and no dubious remark ever fell from their lips. Their friends, who usually belonged to the best society, were noblemen, officers in mufti, industrial magnates, rich idlers, who treated them with every respect, and there was nothing in their conduct to indicate that they were associating with women who lived by love. And yet everyone knew that Mrs So-and-so had a delightful house in the best part of town and was willing to receive there, unceremoniously, any rich man who cared to call."

This new type of woman was a major fashion influence. "Although the ladies of Society did not care to admit it," writes Gertrude Aretz, "it was this new demi-monde which ruled and decided the fashion in matters of elegance. There was indeed nothing new in such a situation, for in matters of this kind the woman who lives by love has always been a pioneer. She is the first to venture on any new extravagance; others follow only when there is no longer any danger of being stared at." The huge cartwheel hats, flower or feather-trimmed, that were all the rage at the beginning of the 1900s were worn first by the elegant demimondaine in the bars. They also wore dresses with a deep décolletage, but it was the hat that played the most important part of the ensemble. The large hats created an air of mystery while the weeping strands of feathers fell on to bare, white shoulders, drawing attention to the décolletage.

Gertrude Aretz notes that "these large befeathered and beflowered hats were very becoming, and added a rakish elegance to the fashionable bars or nightclubs where the gay world of the fin de siècle and the first ten years of the twentieth century supped, danced and

❧ *Coco Chanel is credited with inventing the "Little Black Dress" in the mid-1920s. It quickly assumed that status of an essential item in any woman's wardrobe, one that would take the wearer from day to evening, from office to nightclub. Under Karl Lagerfeld the house of Chanel continues to excel at designing the perfect "LBD".*

During the 1980s the red dress enjoyed a resurgence, in keeping with the optimistic and confident mood of the times. A red dress in sleek jersey, here by Gianfranco Ferre (below), or dynamic spots, such as this jaunty two-piece style by Bill Blass (opposite), announced the wearer as outgoing and a high-achiever.

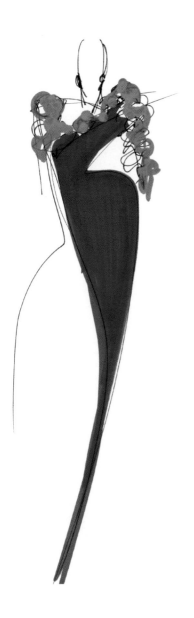

amused itself." Thus the demimondaine of the turn of the century can be considered the forerunners of cocktail style.

The demimondaine was more a creature of Europe than America. Likewise it was European fashion designers who shaped the wardrobes of the American flapper, in particular the cocktail dress. Gabrielle Coco Chanel was one of the most important forces in cocktail fashion. Indeed, her combination of little black dress and costume jewellery, including her signature strings of pearls, has become one of the definitive cocktail looks.

Paul Poiret may have pioneered the loose-waisted dress that did not require corseting, but Chanel took the idea further. She eliminated excess frills, ruffles and matronly leg-of-mutton sleeves in favour of simple lines and shorter hemlines, and used texture and flat decoration such as beadwork to add lustre to evening clothes. The sporty, modern look of her clothing seemed a tailor-made fit for the flapper.

Where World War I saw the demise of Poiret, it saw Chanel prosper. Joshua Zeitz writes that "The war accelerated precisely those trends that made Coco's signature style so appealing. As hundreds of thousands of American, British and French women entered the workforce to help sustain war production … they needed more practical clothes … Strict wartime rationing of raw materials like silk and cotton also inspired a move toward minimalism and simplicity. Out with the pagoda hips and tapered hems [of Poiret] and in with the slender, elegant outline that was favoured at the House of Chanel." As Zeitz notes,

"Chanel was hardly alone in embracing these designs. But she was at the front of the pack — so much so that by 1915 *Harper's Bazaar* had announced that 'the woman who hasn't at least one Chanel is hopelessly out of the running in fashion.'"

Chanel and other French couturiers relied heavily on American clientele during the 1920s, in particular the American department stores that copied and promoted the designers, making their designs affordable for the thousands of fashionable American women who could not afford couture. Cocktail wear was an important part of those designers' collections. However, Elyssa Da Cruz explains that, "As cocktailing had originated in the United States, the French paid less attention to the strict designations of line, cut and length that American periodicals promoted for their *heure de l'aperitif*. While French beach pyjamas gained the most widespread popularity, Louise Boulanger produced *les robes du studio* — chic but rather informal sheaths that suited the hostess of private cocktail gatherings."

Those very wealthy Americans who travelled abroad to chic resorts along the Riviera quickly adopted the new French cocktail styles. But the majority of American women relied on the magazine advertisements in *Vogue* and the selection available in department stores to help them dress for the

Blumarine's satin dress and panne velvet jacket bring to mind the mid-1990s passion for Chinese-style party fashions, fuelled by interest in the Hong Kong handover to China. The cheongsam, collarless jackets with loose sleeves, and lavish embroidery enabled by new mass production embroidery machines, all added to the look.

cocktail hour. Elyssa Da Cruz writes that "though cocktail attire featured the longer sleeves, modest necklines and sparse ornamentation of daytime clothing, it became distinguished by executions in evening silk failles or satins, rather than wool crepes or gabardines. Often the only difference between a day dress and a cocktail outfit was a fabric noir and a stylish cocktail hat."

By 1923 Chanel had established her signature cocktail look — a straight dress with dropped or invisible waistline, high hemline that hovered around the knee, intricate decorative beading and sparkling costume jewellery that could be worn alone or combined with real jewellery. For a working woman, going on to cocktails after work, these all-important accessories made a transformation possible.

"Thanks to me," she once said, working women "can walk around like millionaires." She took the idea one step further in 1926 with the debut of her "little black dress." Cut in matt black crepe, the knee-length dress had a high neckline and long narrow sleeves. *Vogue* magazine's French edition of November that year dubbed it the "uniform of a modern woman." American *Vogue* called it "Chanel's Ford," a comparison to Henry Ford's affordable and accessible mass-produced motor car. "For any girl, any woman with little money, it's marvellous to have the possibility of one dress for the whole season, for the whole year, and be well dressed," wrote the magazine's fashion editor.

Although the designer intended that particular little black dress for daywear, it carried more possibilities

than that for the modern working woman. "What she invented is more a 'principe,' an idea," according to fashion historian and writer Florence Muller, "the fact that a dress can be used in different situations and can be changed by the addition of accessories … Chanel's revolution ushered in the one dress that could be worn from dawn till dusk with little adornment apart from well-chosen costume jewellery, yet remain the ultimate in modern elegance."

Cecil Beaton would look back from the standpoint of the 1950s and suppose that "Perhaps Chanel's genius lay in her intuition that ladies were tired of the finicky trimmings that had been decked upon them for decades. She guessed that women of fashion would be travelling in subways and taxis and would require a new concept. Possibly she turned to nature and rediscovered, or reaffirmed, the fact that the female of the species is generally unadorned, that female birds are drab compared to males. The trick, or the genius, was to convert this drab look into a mode of brilliant simplicity which was exactly what Chanel did. Ruthlessly women were stripped of their finery, fitted with a shirt and skirt or a plain dress; and when they looked like Western Union messenger boys, when they had been reduced to chic poverty, then, and only then did she drape them with costume jewellery, with great lumps of emeralds, rubies, and cascades of huge pearls."

One incarnation of the cocktail party is the late-afternoon pool or patio party, which gained popularity in the 1960s, when people entertained more informally and began vacationing in resorts such as Acapulco and the Bahamas. This 1966 Emilio Pucci "hostess" dress with side split looks tailor-made for a pool or beachside soirée.

Short, sharp and graphic were the overriding principles of the 1960s wardrobe. Emilio Pucci excelled at the mix, winning a devout following and inspiring countless copies. These contemporary cocktail dresses (above and opposite) are by Mathew Williamson for Pucci.

In a way it seemed the antithesis of party dressing to reject the frivolous and embrace the practical, but it was more the proposal of an understated luxury for the cocktail hour that captured women's attention. For perhaps, unlike other evening events, the cocktail party's early starting hour, typically 6pm, requires a more flexible approach. It means, for example, that a woman has to come from the workplace, or from home after getting children ready for bed, with little time for preparation.

This idea, of day into evening clothing, gathered momentum in the following decade. Glynis Ward notes that during the early 1930s, cocktail parties became a common social event. More cocktail entertaining was done at home, as opposed to nightclubs. Hollywood did much to popularise the cocktail party, and cocktail dressing,

According to Elyssa Da Cruz, Chanel, Jean Patou and Elsa Schiaparelli helped to popularise the dressy cocktail suit "as transitional clothing from the afternoon tea to the intimate evening fête." Schiaparelli in particular pioneered the suit for evening, and her witty accessories — hats, shoes, bags — were sought after by fashion enthusiasts for cocktail soirées. Despite her upper class roots, she was very much in touch with the needs of the modern working woman.

The "Dynasty" look dominated evening fashions in the mid-1980s. Like the characters in the soap opera, women wore short straight skirts with fancy jackets in bright colours with lashings of gold. Gianfranco Ferre excelled at the look; his gold sequinned cocktail jacket is from 1986.

As black became the fashion colour for both day and evening clothes, designers of the 1920s found ways of differentiating the two through surface embellishment, often using the new plastic sequins and beads, to make cocktail dresses sparkle. Two modern examples here from Jayson Brundson (opposite) and Escada (above).

Elsa Schiaparelli's husband had left her when their daughter was young, and she set out to make it on her own, with no financial means and rejecting any help from family. Her use of suiting gave her clothes wide appeal, yet her love of art and understanding of the transforming power of clothes were also incorporated into her collections to give them great substance. They were perfectly attuned to cocktail dressing, which needed to be less grand and more practical than formal eveningwear. But it also helped to be wearing engaging and clever clothes that would at the very least set the wearer apart from the sea of black dresses that dominated the cocktail occasion, and would more than likely become a talking point, a means of igniting lively conversation.

Take, for example, Schiaparelli's haute couture "Circus" collection of 1938. Built largely around suiting, with a focus on little silk cocktail jackets and boleros, circus motifs were a central feature. One pink silk twill jacket was patterned with pale blue circus ponies, and had painted metal buttons in the shape of trapeze artists.

Cultural historian Caroline Evans describes the highlights of that collection: "Another cocktail suit with clown-hat buttons was worn with a tall and pointed pink sequinned clown's hat. There were lavishly beaded boleros embroidered with circus elephants spot-lit acrobats, tents and clowns, for which Lesage revived eighteenth-and nineteenth-century military embroidery techniques. The collection also featured the backwards suit, with lapels, buttons, cravat and brooch all on the back. There was a hat that was a nest with a hen sitting on it;

crushed clown top-hats, some with insect brooches; and tall coloured feathers like circus ponies, tied on with ribbons. Shoes were in gold crêpe rubber, and the first platform shoes were worn."

Although exquisitely produced and certainly far beyond the reach of the average working woman, the collection offered clever solutions for the cocktail outfit in its use of bright, wittily decorated pieces — the bolero, the little jacket, the hat, the bag, the shoes — which were a perfect foil for a plain black dress or skirt.

American designers also championed "day-into-evening clothes," favouring "a simple, streamlined silhouette and emphasising the importance of accessories," writes Da Souza. "Cartwheel hats and slouchy fedoras were equally acceptable for the cocktail hour. Gloves, though longer than in the 1930s, continued to be mandatory for late afternoon and evening. Costume jewellery, whether as a daytime pin or an evening parure, became the definitive cocktail accessory."

As it had been in the 1920s, silk remained the desired fabric for cocktail dresses but the cut became more fitted and refined. Tailoring made a strong showing, particularly in the form of little jackets that could be worn either with a skirt or over a dress. Glynis Ward writes that "Tailoring created form-fitting

In the 1930s couturiers such as Chanel and Mainbocher pioneered the use of cotton "day" fabrics for evening, partly in reaction to the austere economic climate. The idea has been revisited by many designers — here Alice McCall uses pink and white gingham for a party dress.

A major change in dress styles occurred around the end of the 1950s as skirts widened and shortened, and, especially for evening, hemlines gained volume. Marchesa's sweet frock (right) finishes in layers of chiffon, while Toni Maticevski's hemline (opposite) is given flounce with a bubble effect.

dresses which were often decorated with rhinestones and lace accents. The 'little black dress' became an essential part of a woman's wardrobe, and the typical cocktail dress colour." But it was not really until after World War II that the cocktail dress came into its own. The year 1947 was a pivotal point in the history of party dressing. Christian Dior's New Look presented a splendid and dramatic vision of womens' dress, sweeping away the dreariness of the war years with his ultra-feminine clothes. Eveningwear was a crucial element of the collection, and was divided into two streams: formal gowns with huge skirts and low-cut, often strapless, bodices; and a new type of dress, the cocktail dress.

According to Gertrud Lehnert in *A History of Fashion in the Twentieth Century*, the cocktail dress was "more dressy than the afternoon dress but less formal than an evening gown because it was never floor length and generally less ornate. Cocktail dresses could be worn at various functions, and under certain circumstances even in the early evening."

Elyssa Da Cruz maintains that "Christian Dior was the first to name the early evening frock a 'cocktail' dress in the late 1940s, and in doing so allowed magazines, department stores, and rival Parisian and American designers to promote fashion with cocktail-specific terminology. Paris *Vogue* included articles entitled 'Pour le cocktail: l'organdi,' while advertisements in *Vanity Fair* celebrated Bemberg's 'cocktail cotton' textiles. Cocktail sets, martini-printed interiors fabrics, and cocktail advertisements all fostered the consumer-driven cocktail culture that had become part of American consciousness by 1960."

Where the cocktail attire of the 1920s and 1930s verged on the practical, Dior's cocktail looks, like most of his other dresses, were unashamedly impractical — worth wearing simply for their sheer femininity and luxurious use of fabric.

High society women embraced his New Look with an enthusiasm that sometimes bordered on the fanatical. In the postwar era women everywhere felt like celebrating, and those with money, often Americans, would celebrate in Dior. Luckily for Monsieur, one of his closest friends and most ardent supporters, Suzanne Luling, was also a brilliant party-throwing, cocktail-sipping, nightclub-hopping advertisement for his designs.

In her book, *Christian Dior: The Man Who Made the World Look New*, Marie-France Pochna describes the effect that Luling had in promoting Dior's cocktail clothes. "As the applause that greeted his first collection gradually subsided," she writes, "Dior fled the capital to seek refuge in an old mill in the countryside, which he had bought with his first earnings. Suzanne Luling, on the other hand, threw open the doors of her Paris apartment on the Quai Malaquais to hold parties that raged until dawn. The strains of gypsy violin or Paraguayan balladeers filled its wood-panelled rooms overlooking the Seine. Suzanne, ever the life of the party, led the dancing. Her 'shindigs' always wound up with a nightclub-hopping session along the Left Bank to places like the Saint-Benoit and Tabou, or even to Monseigneur on Montmartre as the mood took her. She was a veritable queen of the Parisian night … It is hard to imagine Dior without this astonishing, explosive creature at his side."

Thanks in large part to Luling's influence, Dior soon had a blue-ribbon list of clients clamouring for fittings — Princess Margaret, the Duchess of Windsor, Babe Paley, Gloria Guinness, and Elizabeth Taylor among them — and they were more than happy to make the trip to Paris. The City of Light had been reborn as the cultural centre of Europe. It was a magnet for the international moneyed set who had gone underground during the war years, and for wealthy Americans. Paris was also a lively and modern place to be, and the formal entertainment once enjoyed by high society was gradually being replaced with more relaxed cocktail-style events, often in public places such as Maxims, or at galleries and the ateliers of artists and designers.

"Where once high society was out to dinner every night in full evening dress, more potent distractions came to the fore," explains Pochna, "at more vibrant venues, like the theatre, art galleries and fashion houses. The salons at 30 Avenue Montaigne buzzed with a constant stream of clients, none of whom thought twice about circling the globe each season simply to update their wardrobes. They wanted the Dior label, nothing less … The fitting rooms were

A dramatic rise in cocktail hemlines in the early 1960s coincided with a repositioning of the waistline to just below the bust, creating an Empire effect. The overall impression was of a childlike shift, and this short, carefree silhouette became the most fashionable dress for the cocktail hour. Dress by Marchesa.

Marc Bohan and Courrèges were the first couturiers to show minis in 1961, and by 1966 Vogue magazine declared that "Legs are it". One incarnation was the "babydoll", a kind of glorified nightie that became popular for parties. Ruffled babydoll by Tina Kalivas.

the last stop on the social merry-go-round, a perfect place to catch up on the week's events: who was seeing whom, who had broken with whom. No one ever lost sight of the real purpose of the exercise, of course, which was to choose an evening dress other woman would kill for, a plunging neckline he would be unable to resist, or a hat that would leave all the others gasping. Dior's genius offered the perfect tools for seduction."

Full evening dress still had its place, but the cocktail-style ensemble was much in demand. It is interesting to note the proliferation of cocktail outfits from designers of the period, especially Dior. Photographer Willy Maywald recounts an incident at the House of Dior where he was photographing a Swedish model who had recently married a wealthy South American and was now shopping for a wardrobe. At Dior's atelier she encountered Carmel Snow, *Harper's Bazaar* editor, who asked the young woman what she was buying. "Three evening gowns, five cocktail dresses, six coats and twelve suits," she replied. Although Carmel Snow reportedly expressed disbelief that she was not buying more, the list of purchases shows the importance of cocktail attire, compared with conventional eveningwear.

Dior's "Five O'Clock Dress" of 1947 is a classic example of the cocktail dress and the epitome of the New Look. A deep V-neck, slightly off the shoulder and with three quarter sleeves, a tightly cinched waist and gently flared skirt almost to the ankles created a sublime contrast between exposure and coverage. Elbow-length gloves and a felt toque decorated with feathers completed the look. Where the Dior ball gown was a huge affair that often made life difficult for the wearer because of the sheer weight of corseting and fabric layers, the Dior cocktail dress offered the same feminine look and silhouette as grander gowns, but with the advantage of a shorter hemline and delightful matching accessories.

Cocktail dresses often featured bold colours and dramatic flourishes. Dior's "Pisanelle" cocktail ensemble of 1949, named after the Italian Renaissance artist Antonio Pisanello, is a strapless navy blue dress with velvet bodice and silk satin skirt set off with a huge bow at the waist and matching satin coat with voluminous sleeves. Held in the collection of the Metropolitan Museum of Art, the dress is an archetypal example of New Look cocktail wear. As explained in the museum notes that accompany the dress: "The cocktail hour began to represent universal social identities for women: the matron, the wife and the hostess. Cocktail parties rose to the height of sociability, and cocktail clothing was defined by strict rules of etiquette. While invitees were required to wear gloves, the hostess was forbidden the accessory. Guests were obligated to travel to an engagement in a cocktail hat (which had retained the veil made popular in the 1940s), but they were never to wear their hats indoors."

Despite the current acceptance of black as a staple of women's working wardrobes, it has not always been the case. In the 1961 Paris collections, for example, riotous colour ruled for day, and black was only considered chic after 6pm. The little black dress by Gail Sorronda (previous pages) and sleek version by Ferre (opposite) are clearly reserved for evening.

Although the silk velvets and satins in Dior's "Pisanelle" ensemble were more typically used for formal eveningwear prior to the 1950s, as the cocktail party grew in popularity, the strict definition of cocktail wear became more about the way an outfit was accessorised rather than strictly measured in terms of cut and fabric types. Or as the museum description puts it: "Due to the prominence of the cocktail hour in material culture reference, the term 'cocktail dress' was applied on the basis of its accessory items and was no longer dependent on the garment's construction."

Almost a decade later, for his fall/winter collection of 1956, Dior designed what the Metropolitan Museum of Art declared to be "unarguably the 1950s *moderne* of the cocktail hour." The piece in question, "Eventail," is a strapless navy and royal blue striped taffeta dress with a very full skirt. The museum's notes on the dress are as follows: "With a strapless neckline, a rather ostentatious constructive line, and a colourful surface print, the dress would have been rejected for the early evening prior to the 1950s, as its various components belonged (respectively) to late evening or daytime dressing. By mid-century, Parisian couturiers were going to great lengths to enforce an exaggerated formality in order to differentiate themselves from American designers."

The museum description continues with a comparison between the cocktail hostess of the 1950s and the eighteenth-century woman, both of whom could be seen to have used clothing and decoration to convey their social roles. "Here referring to the ubiquitous fans women used to 'communicate' at court, Dior raised the waist but delighted in the fullness of the skirt and the pronounced form of the bust. The fan's role is one to which Dior would have been very sensitive. The aegis and instrument of powerful and coquettish women, it both conceals and discloses. It was, of course, the rigidity of the inner structure emanating from the corset that permitted Dior the license of the strapless gown, just as the décolletage of the eighteenth century was made possible by the shaping of the waist below the platform of bust support." In other words, Dior's dress conjoured up the impression of a fan, which the modern hostess might use in the same way that the eighteenth-century courtier used her fan — to flirt. One can imagine the volume of that skirt moving through the cocktail party, brushing against guests as the wearer passes by, sashaying around the legs but also drawing attention to the bust line from which it fans out.

It is no wonder then that women in 1958 might have had second thoughts about what to wear for a cocktail party. Everything seemed possible, from Dior's "Eventail" frock to Jacques Fath's early evening dress of white organdie, with nipped-in waist and three black velvet bows adorning a bodice that sat high on the throat, to Nina Ricci's short beaded sheath dress with matching taffeta cape.

⟋⟍ Because the cocktail dress is often short in length and streamlined in design, it tends to rely on surface interest for effect. This design by Gabriel Scarvelli is woven from red metallic thread to create a mesh-like appearance that is also quite stiff and more akin to armour than cloth. Little additional interest is required save for a standout necklace.

The back is one of fashion's favourite erogenous zones. Backless dresses first appeared in the early 1930s, inspired in part by the popularity of backless swimsuits, which allowed women to tan more of their bodies. Here the backless dress is edged in ruffles by Bill Blass (opposite) and scooped daringly low by Georges Chakra (above).

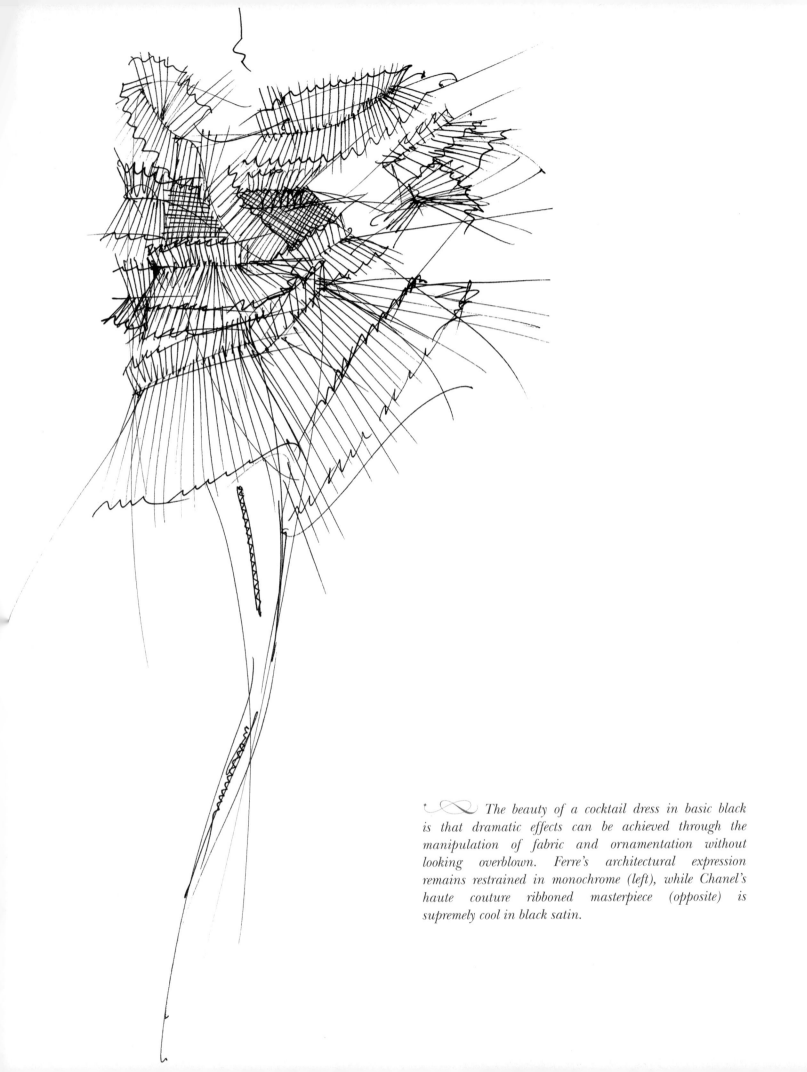

The beauty of a cocktail dress in basic black is that dramatic effects can be achieved through the manipulation of fabric and ornamentation without looking overblown. Ferré's architectural expression remains restrained in monochrome (left), while Chanel's haute couture ribboned masterpiece (opposite) is supremely cool in black satin.

An anecdote from the legendary *Vogue* editor Diana Vreeland helps to demonstrate the extent of some womens' wardrobes for evening. "Have I ever told you about the night I saw Millicent [Rogers, daughter of oil baron H.H. Rogers] at a party at the old Ritz Carlton here in New York?" writes Vreeland in her memoir *DV*. "She started out the evening wearing a dress by Paquin — black silk with a bustle and train. When dessert was served, she spilled some ice cream and left the room to change into another dress. When the coffee was served, she spilled some of that and went off to change into another dress."

As the 1950s progressed, the lines between cocktail and other evening events blurred. Often the cocktail party segued into a dinner, and possibly dancing. One of the style authorities of the times, Genevieve Antoine Dariaux, recognised that there may well be a degree of confusion among women as to what the cocktail dress code entailed, and she was careful to clarify the nature of the event and point out suitable attire for it.

"There is a tendency to confuse cocktail dresses with dinner dresses, although they are not exactly the same," explained Madame Dariaux. "The dress worn by a guest at a cocktail party should be scarcely décolleté at all." However, she also points out that "If the cocktail party is followed by a buffet or sit-down dinner for which you have been invited to stay, the ideal outfit is a dressy ensemble consisting of a low-cut dress worn underneath a co-ordinated or matching coat.

"A cocktail party is the most typical form of contemporary entertaining," she wrote, and did not hesitate to spell out the reasons why it had become so popular. "Much simpler to organise than a dinner, it requires much less imagination and liquidates social obligations to an unlimited number of people with whom you might find it difficult to carry on a conversation during an entire evening. It is a sort of unrecognised receiving line, in which many women enjoy greeting all their friends and acquaintances once a year or once a month."

The social, and political, expediency of the cocktail party has helped to sustain it as one of the most popular forms of evening entertainment. As Genevieve Antoine Dariaux and other commentators have pointed out, the cocktail party served a very valuable function in allowing interaction with a large number of people.

During the London debutante season of the 1950s for example, the cocktail party became a convenient way to meet young men and make dates for balls and other events held later in the season. Fiona MacCarthy, author of *Last Curtsey: The End of the Debutantes*, recalled that "A cocktail party held early in the Season would advertise a girl's credentials and ensure she was invited to the most important dances.

The corseted bodice — shown here in a tiny black dress by Giorgio Armani — has enjoyed renewed popularity since it was revived by Vivienne Westwood and Jean-Paul Gaultier in the 1980s. Although usually considered too restrictive for daywear, it is well suited to statement-making eveningwear.

Girls given cocktail parties in addition to parties in addition to dances had an immediate entrée to the ranks of the top debs."

As editor of American *Vogue*, Diana Vreeland was invited to scores of parties and was aware of the function served by the cocktail party. "One night I was invited to a Condé Nast party. Everybody who was invited to a Condé Nast party stood for something. He was the man who created the kind of social world that was then called Café Society: a carefully chosen mélange — no such thing as an overcrowded room, mind you — mingling with people who up to that time would never have been seen at the same social gathering. Condé picked his guests for their talent, whatever it was — literature, the theatre, big business. Sharp, chic society. Why was I asked? I was young, well dressed, and could dance."

No doubt the self-assured Vreeland could handle herself with aplomb in the most challenging social situations, but for others the cocktail party was a minefield to be negotiated with great care. According to Fiona MacCarthy, the London parties of the debutante "were not for the faint-hearted. Hot and crowded, semi-formal in their dress code with girls in scoop-neck satin, men in uniform dark suits with old school or regimental ties … Once past the greetings line, you were propelled, like the missile from the launcher, into an already thronging, noisy room. Cocktail parties faced the deb with an additional ordeal in that you arrived on your own, unlike dances where you came in a party with the people you had dined with. The first test was in locating somebody you knew and attaching yourself to the group in which they were, edging inwards and joining the conversation as best you could."

The polite etiquette of 1950s behaviour and dress gave way to a sense of freedom in the 1960s, as the youth generation aimed to look as different as possible from their parents. Fashion historian and curator of the Museum at New York's Fashion Institute of Technology, Valerie Steele, notes that "By the early 1960s, if the hostess had a garden or terrace, she might choose to wear a 'patio dress' or 'palazzo pyjamas,' styles that recalled the tea-gowns of the Belle Époque. It was also perfectly acceptable to wear a dressy suit. For those going directly from cocktails to dinner, a matching jacket might be worn over a dinner dress."

Thus the cocktail party came to embrace many types of events, and accordingly dress codes varied widely. Elyssa Da Cruz surmises that "though Pauline Trigère, Norman Norell, and countless Parisian couturiers continued to produce cocktail models well into the next decade, the liberated lines of Galitzine's palazzo pant ensembles and Emilio Pucci's jumpsuits easily replaced the formal cocktail dress in privatised European and American cocktail circuits of the following decades."

Reminiscent of the 1980s puffball, or "pouf" skirt, pioneered by Christian Lacroix, Kate Sylvester's romantic dress combines brocade-effect fabric shot through with metallic thread and a tulle underskirt.

A case in point is one of the social highlights of 1965, an "underground" cocktail party held at The Scene nightclub in Manhattan, hosted in August by Peter Stark, son of film producer Ray Stark, to mark his imminent return to college life. As *Time* magazine reported: "The guest list read like a society columnist's dream: Huntington Hartford, Mrs Eric Javits, Wendy Vanderbilt, Melinda Moon, Freddie Guest (Winston's son), and his wife Stephanie (Joan Bennett's daughter), Maria Cooper (Gary's daughter), Liza Minelli (Judy's daughter), Alexandra Cushing and Christina Paolozzi, plus a constellation of Southampton and Newport debs, some of whom flew in for the occasion, But all eyes were on Edie and Andy."

The Edie and Andy referred to in the article were Edie Sedgwick and Andy Warhol. Edie was dressed in her "uniform" of black fishnets and tight black hotpants, a blue surfer's shirt and huge earrings, and she danced under the studio lights with the rest of the Warhol entourage. Andy, meanwhile was filming the scene. "After several paper cups full of champagne and cider, the socialites unbuttoned their suit jackets, set their ties at half mast, and mixed it up with the denizens of the undergound on the dance floor," noted *Time* magazine's columnist. "Said one girl in a

❧ "Understated luxury" has become the most sought after quality in contemporary cocktail wear. Blumarine's relaxed styles employ beautiful fabrics and delicate details (left). Chanel's example in stiff faille is made luxurious with the addition of a beaded sash (overleaf, left). Chaiken's dress (overleaf, right) is based on the style of a summer dress but wrought in silk with a lace-edged skirt.

JEFF MAHSHIE FOR CHAIKEN M.L.P GOLDEN GLOBES 06

Since the dress reform movement of the late nineteenth century, which lobbied for an end to the corset, comfort and practicality have become increasingly important concerns, even for special occasion clothing. Stretch fabrics, shorter hemlines and looser lines, as in Filippa K's graphic dress, for example, have all helped.

Pucci gown: 'This is a gas! I mean, this is what I call a real party!'"

In the 1970s, American designer Halston reinvented cocktail wear for a new generation. Often worn at nightclubs and discos, as much as private drinks parties, his soft jersey tunics and halter dresses became *the* look for the early evening hours, which often extended well into the early morning. Valerie Steele writes: "He designed silk caftans for clients like Babe Paley and Marie-Helene de Rothschild; jersey halter-jumpers for Liza Minelli and Lauren Bacall …" Indeed Halston was responsible for the cult of the caftan and, in the words of Patricia Mears, "revamped the thirties pajama into cocktail and evening clothes by making his pajamas of silk charmeuse and adding a plunging neckline."

In contrast to the fluid styles of the late 1970s, the 1980s heralded a return to formal cocktail dressing. Christian Lacroix became famous for his bouffant or "pouf" cocktail dresses in luxurious fabrics and jewel colours. Karl Lagerfeld at Chanel reinvented the little black dress and the cocktail suit, with liberal use of gold buttons, chains and costume jewellery.

In current times, the definition of cocktail attire is open to many interpretations. As an invention of modern twentieth-century culture its history is relatively brief. The only certain thing that can be said is that the term "cocktail" embraces all things not strictly formal, whether a party at a nightclub or gallery exhibition opening. Dress codes are no longer religiously adhered to and can vary from jeans to a vintage couture frock. Perhaps the only reliable guide to the cocktail party is *Debrett's Etiquette and Modern Manners*, which simply outlines the starting time, and the drinks that should be served.

Debrett's would surely concur with the opinion of American essayist and satirist Russell Baker who bemoaned the decline of the cocktail, and the trend of drinking imported mineral waters: "Social historians will date the decline of the cocktail party from the summer of 1975, when chic people first asked for 'a little white wine with soda and ice,' instead of the traditional rum, whisky or gin." Saddened by what he described as 'ostensibly sane people turning up at parties and ordering water,' Baker concluded that "If Americans were able to let their hair down over imported water, Prohibition might have succeeded. The cocktail party surely would never have been invented, no man would have ever insulted his boss, no woman would ever have been indiscreet … I miss all these things at the imported-water parties nowadays, with their dedicated guests on lonesome pursuits sturdily keeping their hair up. Next morning of course there is a clear head but very little worth remembering in life."

❧ *Coco Chanel endeavoured to imbue all her designs with simplicity and a cut that allowed a woman freedom to move. "Luxury must be comfortable, otherwise it is not luxury," she once said. Karl Lagerfeld remains true to the Chanel vision with his knife-pleated maxi dress (opposite). La Perla's little cocktail dress (overleaf) draws on the design label's lingerie expertise to create a garment that looks polished but feels as light as a negligee.*

Dressing for a cocktail party in the twenty-first century offers unlimited possibilities, whether a romantic black dress or a sharp tuxedo suit (previous pages), both Carla Zampatti; a fitted dress in magenta (opposite), by Tina Kalivas, or Collette Dinnigan's bejewelled slip (right).

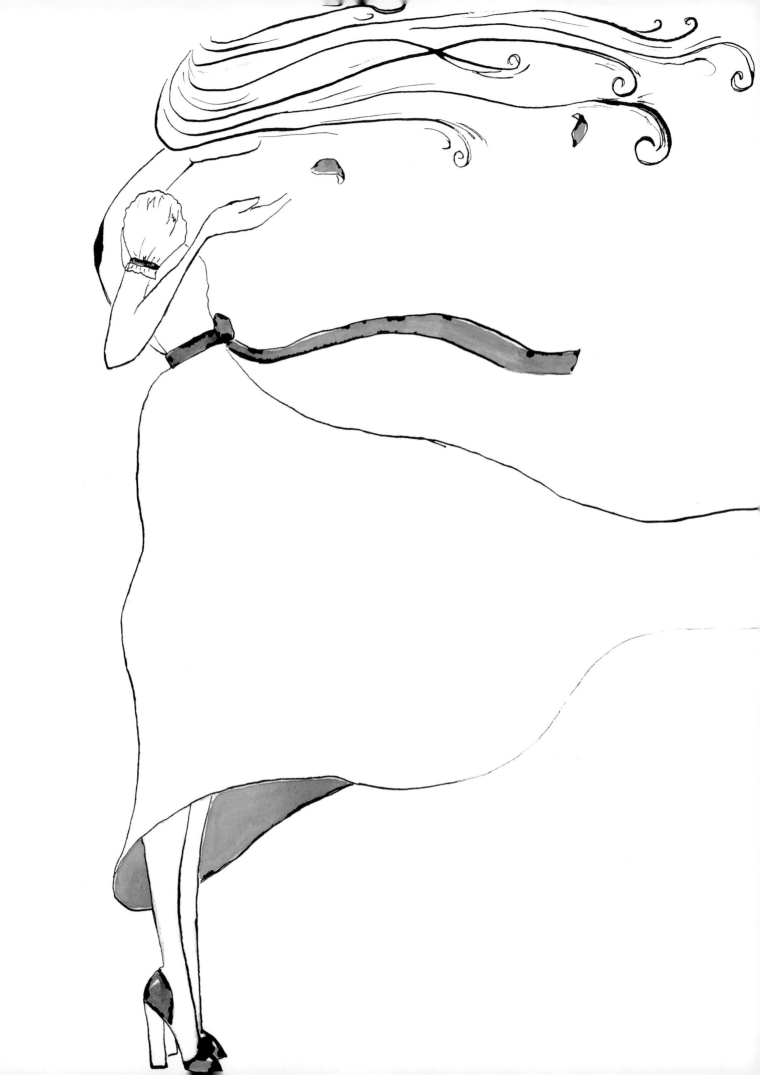

Chapter Four

The Garden Party

"They could not have had a more perfect day for a garden party if they had ordered it. Windless, warm, the sky without a cloud. Only the blue was veiled with a haze of light gold, as it is sometimes in early summer."

Katherine Mansfield, The Garden Party

The garden is a place of fantasy. With its serene arbours, manicured lawns, trimmed hedges, flower beds and ordered plantings, the ideal garden allows humans to experience nature at its most charming, without threat or discomfort. It is no surprise then that the garden is also a favoured setting for entertainment. The garden party provides an opportunity for the enjoyment and appreciation of nature in a controlled manner, and of course allows the host to show off his or her talents in having cultivated such a beautiful place.

At various times throughout history the garden has been considered a place of religious significance, of pure pleasure, of enlightenment, or of good health. In medieval times the garden served a predominantly practical purpose, as a place for growing fruit, vegetables and herbs. It did have some ornamental features such as parterres, paths, orange and lemon trees in terracotta pots and a small fountain or fish pond. But it was not until a few hundred years later, at the height of the Renaissance, that the idea took hold of the garden as a setting for socialising.

One of the earliest recorded European garden parties was Titian's summer garden party of 1540. The occasion was *ferrare agosto*, a religious holiday celebrated in Italy with great vigour, nowhere more

The origins of the garden party are grounded in the Renaissance idea of the garden as an extension of the house, designed for appreciation and enjoyment. Garden party fashions are typically romantic and draw on nature for inspiration. Shades of white, floral prints and petal colours are de rigueur. Fashion photograph from the 1950s by Cecil Beaton.

so than Venice. The painter Titian, literary sensation of the day Pietro Arentino and the influential architect Jacopo Tatti, called Sansovino, had decided to escape the crowds in Venice on the night of *ferrare agosto,* and enjoy a private party of their own in Titian's extensive garden. With its superb view of the Lagon of Venice and the islands of Murano and San Michele, it was an idyllic setting for a hot summer's night. The trio had invited their friends, the cultural elite of the city.

Guests began arriving in the afternoon when the sun was still hot and bright. Among them was the Florentine grammarian Francesco Priscianese, who recorded that the charming garden setting evoked "singular pleasure and a note of admiration from all of us." He recalled that "before the tables were set out, because the sun, in spite of the shade, still made its heat much felt, we spent the time in looking at the lively figures in the excellent pictures, of which the house was full."

As the sun set, preparations were made for the feast. One guest recalled, "It was the hour when sunset had embroidered all the West with a thousand variety of clouds; some violet, some darkly blue and a certain crimson; others between yellow and black, and few so burning with fire of backward-beaten rays that they seemed as though of polished and finest gold."

❧ Society beauty and novelist Nancy Mitford grew up in an aristocratic seventeenth-century English country house in the Windrush Valley, Oxfordshire — Asthall Manor, which is known for its picturesque grounds. In this photographic portrait she conjures up the simple delights of summer in the garden, albeit against a studio backdrop.

In planning his party, Titian may have been reminded of a magnificent garden fête he had attended in Ferrara at the invitation of Ippolito II, Cardinal d'Este. The party began with a play and concert. Then, as described in Carolin C. Young's *Apples of Gold in Settings of Silver,* "dancers and musicians accompanied fifty-four distinguished guests to the head table. Foliate festoons and trophies were strung overhead. A stacked credenza stood at one side, lending décor and facilitating service; entertainers performed in a leafy thicket on the other side. Salads of herbs garnished with festively cut lemons, of spinach, and of anchovies; dishes of pignoli nuts; and small plates of sturgeon fritters had been laid out on the table, amidst scattered flowers and miniature emblems of the Este coat of arms. Sugar sculptures of Venus, Bacchus, and Cupid marked the occasion as a glorious bacchanal. The party sat down to eat at ten o'clock in the evening and finished consuming eighteen courses of eight dishes each at five o'clock in the morning."

Although Titian's own party was certainly not on the scale of the cardinal's, he was renowned for his elegance, and Priscianese described the supper as "no less beautiful and arranged than copious and well provided. Besides the most delicate viands and precious wines there were all those pleasures and amusements that are suited to the season, the guests and the feast."

After sunset, gazing out on the water, guests enjoyed pleasures of a different kind, as Priscianese writes: "This part of the sea, as soon as the sun went down, swarmed with gondolas, adorned with beautiful

women, and resounded with the varied harmony and music of voices and instruments, which till midnight accompanied our delightful supper." All the elements were present for the perfect garden party: balmy summer weather, an elegant outdoor setting, good food and wine, music and good company.

The Italians have a long history of outdoor parties and their predecessors the Romans were notoriously fond of outdoor celebrations in bacchanalian spirit. The Italian concept of al fresco entertaining had certainly found its way to the French courts by the seventeenth century, and there were few places better suited to a garden party than the Palace of Versailles, with its splendid landscaped grounds. One of the most famous parties in its history took place in 1664 when the young King Louis XIV, then just twenty-six years old, staged a week-long garden party involving some 600 guests. The King was a lover of the outdoors, more at home in the fields and woods than in the tapestry hung corridors of the palace, so it made sense for him to entertain his courtiers in an environment where he felt at his most inspired. The party officially began on May 7 at six in the evening, with an enchanting outdoor spectacle, set in the natural arena where four great tree-lined avenues intersected. The area was bounded by yews and further defined by four faux triumphal gateways, erected especially for the occasion, that opened on to the magical vistas of the garden. However, as always with a garden party, the success of the event turned on the weather.

Historian John Russell writes that on the appointed evening, "The weather was dry, but windy, and it seemed possible that the *maître des plaisirs*, the Duc de Saint Aignan, and his Modenese technical advisor, Carlo Vigarani, had devised too fragile or too hasty a framework for the fête. What if the candles — of which 4,000 were lit every evening — were all to be blown out? What if the decorations, the momentary palaces of lath and canvas were to collapse upon the guests? Anxiety proved pointless. All marched according to plan. The six hundred, wearied perhaps of ordinary dances, and with their ingenuity taxed by the masked balls of the preceding years, sat out three evenings of exemplary stage management."

The theme for the evening was taken from the poet Ariosto's *Les Plaisirs de I'Ile Enchantée* which tells of the "pleasures" dreamt up by a beautiful sorceress, Alcina, to amuse her captive, Roger and his attendant nights. The climax of the story is Roger's rescue by Melise. As John Russell notes, "Saint-Aignan was too good a courtier to forget that Louis XIV's great skill as a horseman would have to be exploited throughout the entertainment; and so it was that horses and horsemanship played perhaps a greater part in the life of the enchanted island than Aristo had envisaged."

The flower is the focal point of any garden, and at a garden party women customarily dress to mimic its beauty and delicacy (opposite). The Edwardian lady dressed for a garden party in ruffled lace, as recreated by actress Diana Wynyard (overleaf, left), while in the early 1930s trailing chiffon and feathers were favoured (overleaf, right).

In due course, the guests seated in the outdoor arena were suitably impressed by the lavishly costumed spectacle of the King as Roger on horseback, and all the characters of the story, likewise bedecked in glittering outfits, portrayed by members of the court. The evening ended with a formal supper lit by green and silver candlesticks bearing two hundred wax candles. Screens of foliage were erected around the midnight banquet to protect both guests and candles from the breeze. The next evening as John Russell describes it, "it was the turn of Molière to entertain the visitor. *The Princesse d'Elide* is not a good play, but in the theatre which Vigarani had created in the gardens of Versailles, in which the traffic of the stage merged imperceptibly into the dream-vistas of the canals beyond, and before an audience alert to the mischief of Molière's every allusion, it was enjoyed as few plays are enjoyed." On the final evening after yet another theatrical spectacle, this great garden party climaxed with a spectacular fireworks display.

Although there would have been no special dress code at such an event to distinguish it as a garden party, as opposed to any other formal court entertainment,

in the next century another French royal would give the garden party a less formal, more relaxed style, which was reflected in fashion as well.

Despite Marie Antoinette's reputation for lavish spending on luxurious clothes, shoes and jewellery, the young Queen also developed a taste for simple, pastoral pleasures and the delights of the garden. The setting for her garden-themed entertainments was the Petit Trianon, a small neoclassical chateau not far from Versailles. A month after acceding to the throne Louis XVI gave the country palace to Marie Antoinette, knowing her desire to escape from the rituals and pressures of court life at Versailles.

The Queen was enchanted with her new retreat with its delicate lines, intimate spaces and floral-themed decoration, and used this setting to build a particular way of life that resembled a pastoral idyll. Caroline Weber writes in *Queen of Fashion* that "Struck by the Petit Trianon's freshness and simplicity, the Queen promptly and enthusiastically set about transforming the place into a laboratory for a program of broad-based aesthetic and cultural experimentation. From the gardens to the interiors, and from the costumes she and her invited guests wore to the kinds of activities and behaviours she encouraged there, Marie Antoinette designed virtually every aspect of life at her villa along the understated, informal lines suggested by its architecture. Taken together, her innovations established a domain where none of the courtly rules applied …"

Indeed, from her base at Petit Trianon Marie Antoinette began to forge another revolution in fashion as influential as the powdered wigs and elaborate costumes she had preferred earlier.

As the author goes on to explain, the young Queen was also tapping into social currents of the times. "Chief among these currents," she notes, "was the tradition of the pastoral — the so-called cult of the simple life — which had long held an important place in French literary and courtly life. Perhaps most notably, in the seventeenth century, aristocrats enamoured of the long, bucolic novel *Astraea*, had staged elaborate performances, disguised as the shepherds and shepherdesses that the book introduced as its protagonists. A century later, the ideal of a natural existence, unspoiled by the corrupting elements of modern life, had very much returned to favour, thanks above all to the Swiss-born philosopher and novelist Jean-Jacques Rousseau."

It is not too much of a stretch to suppose that the enduring popularity of the garden party taps into this wish, for a return to nature, and a simpler, freer way of life. However, as Marie Antoinette demonstrated with such élan, the pastoral theme could be carried off with great style and a large measure of luxury. To prepare her new retreat for the sort of lifestyle she wanted, she carried out numerous interior changes, and perhaps, most importantly, she altered the grounds, replacing the formal, ordered landscaping

The concept of the rural idyll was revived in the 1960s for the "flower power" generation, sparking a passion for romantic clothes, typically white, and adorned with daisies or incorporating lace insets. Cecil Beaton's 1965 photograph, including "it" models Jean Shrimpton and Celia Hammond, captures the look.

of Louis XIV's reign with a romantic *jardin anglais* of meadows, casual groupings of trees and flowering plants and even a rotunda, which she called the "Temple of Love", built on a tiny island planted with lilacs and roses.

To celebrate the completion of the "Temple of Love" Marie Antoinette threw a royal garden party in September 1777, which she planned in meticulous detail. It was, according to Caroline Weber, "conceived as a fête galante — a relaxed outdoor idyll of the sort made famous in the paintings of Antoine Watteau…" The party was set in a mock village square with fairgrounds, a marketplace with food stalls, and even a tavern where ladies of the court poured drinks and the Queen herself took charge of dispensing lemonade to her guests.

The dress code for this and later festivities at Petit Trianon, although far less grand than required at Versailles, was nevertheless carefully thought out by Marie Antoinette and she went to considerable efforts to make sure that her attire, and that of her visitors, fitted with the bucolic mood of her surrounds. When her childhood friend, the Princess Louis von Hesse Darmstadt came to visit, Marie Antoinette wrote to her in advance to "kindly request that you not come in formal attire, but rather in country wear." Hoops, whalebone corsets and diamonds were banned.

The bohemian-style maxi dress was a variant of garden party fashions in the late 1960s and early 1970s, when entertaining outdoors took on a more informal tone.

Instead, the Queen and her ladies wore long gowns of muslin and cambric, simply decorated with a lace kerchief pinned at the breast and topped with large straw hats or cloth bonnets trimmed with ribbons and flowers.

Inspired by their romantic surroundings the ladies at Trianon modelled their appearance to resemble wildflowers. As Caroline Weber explains, "To achieve this effect, they traded imposing gemstones for pretty lilac spangles; gigantic furbelows for silk flowers and ribbons (fittingly known as *gaze reine* or 'the Queen's gauze'); flashy gemstones for rustic metal jewellery and homespun, if often expensive, muslin kerchiefs or fichus."

Her choice of colours became particularly significant as Marie Antoinette developed her new country look. Traditionally the French elite wore rich, vivid jewel-like colours as a way of declaring their status. But at Trianon, the Queen gravitated towards lighter colours, in particular the neutrals of white, beige and grey, as well as pretty pastels. She also enjoyed wearing delicate patterns such as tiny spots and florals, in contrast to the grandiose patterns favoured at Versailles. Interestingly the palette of colours and the types of patterns worn by Marie Antoinette at her garden retreat are still the favoured choices for modern-day garden parties. Even so the Queen still made concessions to her previous love of large "pouf"-style hairdos, but for parties at Petit Trianon she made efforts to give them a "natural" theme. One lady of the court, Frau von Oberkirch, recounted how in 1782 she attended a party at Trianon, for which she started preparing at six in the morning:

I was experimenting at that time with a very modern but extremely uncomfortable coiffure. For the latest invention of fashion was to wear little tubes filled with water arranged in the hair, so that all the live flowers used to decorate it might remain fresh. It is true that this was not always successful, but, when it was, it gave the charming effect of early spring, with fresh flowers pushing their heads through the snow of the powdered hair.

According to fashion historian Gertrude Aretz, "Marie Antoinette also wore one of these coiffeurs on the occasion in question, but particular envy was felt of another lady of the court for her very unusual mode of hairdressing. She wore in her hair a small gaily coloured bird made of precious stones which at every movement hopped up and down, for it was attached to a fresh rose by a wire, so that it appeared to be hovering perpetually about the head of its lovely wearer."

The age of extravagance that marked Marie Antoinette's reign would very soon be at an end, to be replaced by the new age of the Directoire. But

The floating chiffon dresses designed for the character of Daisy Buchanan in the 1974 film of F. Scott Fitzgerald's The Great Gatsby, *highlighted the character's fragility, and also took into consideration Mia Farrow's pregnancy.*

the simplicity of dress and the naturalism of dress pioneered by the Trianon ladies was taken up to the extreme by the post-Revolutionary women of fashion in France. Once again there was a strong connection with nature and the outdoors, which can be seen as precedents for styles of garden party dress. Fashion took as its starting point the reverence for nature of ancient times, and then ran with the idea to create a new look.

Inspired by Greek and Roman mythology and history, the women of Paris stripped off their heavy silk robes, layers of petticoats and corsets, to display their bodies freely in light dresses that showed the female form, often leaving little to the imagination. Gertrude Aretz maintains that "The *merveilleuses* and nymphs of the Directory displayed an exaggeration and extravagance in their elegance which has kept their name alive. Anything Greek or Roman was in fashion, and too many mistook the merely nude for the really classical. Dresses were worn with no sleeves, displaying the bare arms; the shoe gave place to the cothurnus, or, better still, to a mere sole with straps. Petticoats and chemises were discarded, and *sans-chemise* became the echo of *sans-culottes*. The breasts were pressed up by a kind of bust-bodice, and were sometimes quite bare, without any neckerchief or fichu. The corset, which had a short time ago played so big a part, fell out of fashion; it was even denounced by politicians in the Assembly as 'injurious to the nation', and its abolition was urged. Mme Hamelin carried the craze for scanty raiment so far that she appeared on the streets one day in nothing but a robe of tulle."

This dramatic change in fashion was of course a way in which women could distance themselves from what they considered the excesses of Louis XVI's reign (although the Queen herself had championed a simpler style of dress). It also signalled an interest in classical times and in humanity's relationship with nature. In the same vein, the idea of the garden as a backdrop for social interaction and entertainment, enjoyed a resurgence.

As Gertrude Aretz explains, "The new freedom brought in by the Revolution allowed women to appear not only at balls and at the theatre, at parties and in the so-called *bureaux d'esprit*, where they mixed with men of letters and politicians, but also in the public gardens and promenades, where they revealed themselves, in the summer, half naked under the dark trees, in shrubberies and grottoes, by the fountains and cascades illuminated with thousands of lanterns of all imaginable colours. Women displayed, as so often in ages of licence, a remarkable mixture of naturalness and affectation."

As an expression of this new approach to nature, and awareness of human connection to it, public gardens, and the pastime of strolling in them, were all the rage, not only in Paris but most especially in

Designer Carolina Herrera, born into an old Venezuelan-family, grew up in grand style and knows how to dress properly for any occasion. Pictured here in 1974 with her husband Reinaldo at the family estate, the 65-room Hacienda La Vega in Caracas, she projects the garden party aesthetic with characteristic flair.

London, where the English passion for gardens was unrivalled. The capital boasted Hyde Park, which in the late seventeenth century was, according to Gertrude Aretz, "the accepted rendezvous of beauty and fashion," and Kensington Gardens, which became the fashionable spot for promenading in the eighteenth century. "Here strolled and chatted the beaux and belles of society," continues Aretz. "Here women displayed their toilettes and their beauty, flirted with the men, and showed off their fine carriages. At times there were as many as a thousand on the long drive from Kensington to Hyde Park Corner, the ladies sitting behind the clear plate-glass windows like so many lovely pictures framed and glazed … This driving and promenading in the London parks lasted only for a short summer season — from May to August."

Certainly in northern climates, garden parties were restricted to these few short months. The English in particular embraced garden entertainments wholeheartedly and they became a fixture of the summer season. It was as if spring and summer not only heralded the reawakening of the garden and blooming of flowers, it was also an opportunity for women to emerge from the darkness of winter and show off in pretty, light colours and romantic clothing. The garden party remained a firm favourite of London hostesses into the late 1800s particularly at country homes where there was space to cultivate a truly beautiful garden setting.

The Victorian-era coincided with an enormous interest among Europeans in plants from other parts of the world, and garden parties became especially important as collectors and gardeners sought to show off their prize flowers. Public subscription garden fêtes were also popular in the summer months, such as the one organised by the Royal Horticultural Society on June 23, 1827. Held in the Society's garden at Chiswick, the event attracted 2,843 guests to view the gardens and a special exhibition of fruit, accompanied by refreshments and music provided by a military band. Garden parties were a great opportunity for women to enjoy a social event that did not dictate the usual separation of men and woman, as was often the case at formal dinners or balls, when women were often obliged to retire early. This first RHS fête was deemed a huge success, and the committee notes recorded that "It was allowed by all parties that such an assemblage of women of beauty, fashion, and rank, had never before been seen in a garden."

The following year, the RHS fête was one of the popular garden events of the year and went off without a hitch. But good weather is essential for the success of any garden party, and the Society's 1929 efforts were dashed by bad weather despite elaborate preparations. A long line of tents had been erected all the way along the gravel walkway that wound through the grounds. These were to serve as a promenade if the weather was fine, and provide shelter if it

A winsome dress by designer Gabriel Scarvelli, with its stylised pansy print and butterfly sleeves, recalls the 1930s and Madeleine Vionnet's invention of the bias cut. Historically, a dress for a garden party was made to respond to movement because dancing was often part of the proceedings. The dance floor and orchestra were typically positioned in a tent or marquee in case of rain.

The face-framing, wide-brimmed picture hat is a well-established element of garden party dress, as stylishly displayed in Cecil Beaton's fashion photograph of the 1950s (opposite) and by Lady Pamela Gelconner (above, at left) hosting a garden party at Admiral's House in Hampstead, London, in July 1935.

rained. Five tents were set up for refreshments, with "tables extending for a thousand feet in length for the viands," according to the Society's journal. Music came courtesy of the Royal Artillery "in their beautiful white uniforms" by day, and the Tyrolese Minstrels and Les Trois Troubadours in the evening.

The Society's journal concluded that the day "had all the elements of the grandest fête; and had the weather been equally favourable it would have been a spectacle equal to the proudest days in the annals of George the Fourth ... The doors opened at one o'clock, at which time a long line of equipages graced the high Hammersmith-road, nearly fifteen hundred in number, and extending to Hyde Park corner." There was a little light drizzle but nothing to put off the fashionable throng as they paraded around the garden, admiring among other new plants the now well-known annual *Clarkia pulchella*. However, just after four in the afternoon a terrible storm blew up and thoroughly drenched those party guests not already ensconced in the marquees, and they could only watch helplessly as shoes were lost, and dresses were sullied in the water and mud. Some of the men braved the elements to dash to the caterer's tent, returning to the ladies in the marquees bearing in their umbrellas "dishes containing whole chickens, tongues, &c., together with an abundance of fruit," while others "conveyed Champagne, Burgundy, Claret and Madeira."

Popular cartoonist of the day Paul Pry recorded the party in an illustrated plate under the title, "The Horticultural Fate." It depicts the garden party fashions of the day, which for women included dresses with long, voluminous sleeves, tiny waists and bell-shaped skirts. Hemlines often stopped short at the ankle to allow easier movement than a full-length hemline and also to reveal dainty slippers tied with ribbons. An enormous picture hat adorned with bows and feathers was considered de rigueur for an English garden fête. In this case, unfortunately, the guests are shown in the deluge running for cover, or attempting to stand on tree roots or stumps to keep their shoes and clothes out of the muddy water. Below the image, the cartoonist had written: "Our gayness and gear are all besmirched."

Although the Victorian era had awakened popular interest in the garden, it was really the Edwardian age that saw garden parties flourish. As Cecil Porter writes in his book of Edwardian etiquette *Not Without a Chaperone*, "They called the pre-1914 Belle Epoque the Casino and Garden Party Period. Glancing over the plates of Casino Toilettes in the fashion papers, the aspiring Edwardian Lady may have dreamed for a moment of being a diamond-hung, frothy-petticoated *poule de luxe* in alluring 'Monte' [Carlo] ... Then with a jolt she would recall that she was living ... in Wimbledon and that she must not forget to invite the vicar to her garden party."

Ruffles and frills have often featured in fashion when ultra-feminine looks have been in vogue, and are ideal decorative features for a garden party dress. Examples here by Mat Pal (previous pages) and Collette Dinnigan (opposite).

In the words of Emily Post, writing in her style guide of the 1920s, a garden party "may be as elaborate as a sit-down wedding breakfast or as simple as a miniature strawberry festival." Consequently dress styles vary widely, from sweet and restrained to fun and freewheeling such as this exuberant print dress by Etro.

The floral print dress has always been a popular
choice for garden parties as it fits the setting exactly, whether
Carven's delicate, romantic design from the 1950s (above)
or Luca Luca's bold and colourful style (opposite).

Indeed the garden party was a popular choice for the Edwardian hostess as it allowed her to entertain a large number with relative ease, in a similar way that the cocktail party allowed in the mid-twentieth century. One social commentator of the day, Mrs Danvers Delano, wrote in her 1914 book *The Ways of Society*: "A great many people, particularly in the country, are too uninteresting to entertain except at a garden party, and they look forward from year to year to their annual outings." Cecil Porter surmised that "Those parties on velvet lawns amid the luscious fragrant tea roses, seemed to be bathed in the light of an eternal afternoon with silk and lace confections, shiny toppers, the band tiddly-pom-pomming the latest numbers from San Toy or The Arcadians, the tinkle of teaspoons in the water-ice glasses. There a Lady could unbend without the social obligations of the dinner party."

The garden party of the late nineteenth century and early twentieth century seems to be very much an English phenomenon. Visiting England in 1911, Pierre de Coulevain wrote in his book *The Unknown Isle*: "At this season of the year in England there are garden parties everywhere. It is the special distraction of the season, a distraction of British invention. These outdoor receptions allow hostesses to invite a great many people at the same time. Some of these people are not invited to more intimate receptions, so that it is a way of getting rid of certain social obligations.

"Another thing about this form of entertainment," the author continues, "is that it looks much more than it really costs. For garden parties to be a success, there ought to be a park and planty of trees, green velvety lawns, footmen in handsome livery, and all kinds of luxurious accessories, plenty of beautiful, well-dressed women and distinguished-looking men .... At Wimbledon there always seems to be one of these parties going on. We see files of carriages, nearly every day, in front of some house and the music of more or less Hungarian orchestras can be heard. Out in the green lanes, we meet ladies and young girls, arrayed in light dresses and flower-trimmed hats. It appears that such little festivities are very easily arranged."

Garden parties varied enormously in terms of grandeur and scale, depending on the status of the host, although there was a universal understanding of both the dress code and party essentials. For women, a light-coloured dress, preferably lace-trimmed, and large hat with feathers or flowers and sometimes a veil as well, gloves and a parasol. For gentlemen, morning suit and top hat. Live music provided by a band or orchestra set the mood, while food and drinks were supposed to be as vast and varied as possible. According to Lady Colin Campbell in her 1911 publication *Etiquette of Good Society*, even the hostess of a modest garden party should at least consider: "cold roast beef, ribs and shoulder of lamb,

The floral "hostess" dress is typically a slim, loose shift printed with large, bright blooms. It was highly popular in the 1960s for outdoor entertaining. As its name implies, it was often worn by the hostess of the party who, according to etiquette, should be dressed more informally than her guests. However, the history of the bold floral print dates to the late fifteenth century when nobles of the Flemish and Burgundian courts wore Venetian silks with huge floral designs.

roast fowls, ducks, ham, pressed tongue, beefsteak, pigeon and grouse pies, game, veal patties, lobsters, cucumbers and lettuces for salad, cheesecakes, jam or marmalade turnovers, stewed fruit in bottles, bottle of cream, college puddings, blancmange in mould, plain biscuits to eat with fruit and cheese, rolls, butter, cream cheese, and fresh fruit. Bottled beer and porter, claret, sherry, champagne, soda-water, lemonade and cherry brandy ..."

If Lady Colin Campbell were to elaborate on the types of fruit most suitable for offering at a garden party, strawberries would almost certainly top the list. Pierre de Coulevain observed that although the garden parties of the middle classes and the upper classes might be very different, "the rites and ceremonies are the same, though, the shaking hands with the hosts, the chattering in groups, the flirtation when possible, the tea with all kinds of dainties, but always accompanied by strawberries and cream, and often champagne." The popularity of this latter combination was such that the writer concluded: "I used to think that garden parties had been created thanks to lawns, but I fancy it was thanks to the strawberries and cream and champagne."

Few other cultures seem to have embraced the ritual of the formal garden party with as much passion as

Flowers have long served as a source of inspiration for both artists and designers. The cornflower, Centaurea cyanus — *once prized for its blue pigment, and in folklore worn by men in love — informs designer Lisa Ho's summer dress (opposite). Her exotic design (previous pages) with its colours of orange, red, blue and green brings to mind the tropical Bird of Paradise,* Strelitzia reginae.

the British. The garden party was certainly a feature of American high society, particularly in the Eastern town of Newport, Rhode Island, where America's wealthiest families spent the summer. Garden fêtes were a common occurrence during the season there and usually dictated extremely formal dress despite the hot weather. Typical attire for ladies included tight corsets, white muslin dresses with ornate embroidery, ostrich feather hats with veils, gloves and parasols. Similarly in British colonies such as Australia, India and parts of East Africa the custom of the garden party was entrenched. They were an essential part of the social program when royals or dignitaries came to visit.

The garden party has endured in many of these places, but especially in England, where its most famous incarnation is the royal garden party held each year at Buckingham Palace. Dress codes now differ wildly, from the conventional floral or pastel chiffon or silk dress with hat to far more casual dress, which would horrify the ladies of the Edwardian era. Even *Debrett's Modern Etiquette and Manners* offers just a few lines to guide contemporary garden-party goers. "The traditional garden party is essentially a buffet tea with alcoholic refreshments. It begins about 3.30pm and usually ends shortly after 6pm … Clothes at a traditional garden party are rather formal and elegant. Men wear lounge suits and women tend to wear smart afternoon dresses and,

if they wish, hats. Women should be practical when deciding what shoes to wear; very narrow heels will sink into a lawn." For a Royal Garden Party, *Debrett's* notes that "The majority of women wear afternoon dresses and hats, or national dress."

For many people, the most evocative image of the garden party is that drawn in Katherine Mansfield's short story, *The Garden Party*, published in 1922. In her depiction of a garden fête at her parents' home, the main character, Laura Sheridan, finds solace from the discomfort of the real world in the utopian realm of the garden. And so the story concludes:

The band struck up; the hired waiters ran from the house to the marquee. Wherever you looked there were couples strolling, bending to the flowers, greeting, moving on over the lawn. They were like bright birds that had alighted in the Sheridans' garden for this one afternoon, on their way to — where? Ah, what happiness it is to be with people who all are happy, to press hands, press cheeks, smile into eyes … And the perfect afternoon slowly ripened, slowly faded, slowly its petals closed.

For a summer garden party, Emily Post's Etiquette *of 1922 advised that "if you have very few clothes, you can perfectly well wear any sort of day dress that may be in fashion." But she warned that "a coat and skirt is not appropriate, since a skirt and shirt-waist is and always has been a utility combination." Peter Som's collection of smart summer dresses would no doubt have met with her approval.*

Chapter Five

The Wedding Party

"Well it's, it's what every girl dreams of. A bridal dress, the orange blossoms, the music. It's something lovely to remember all the rest of her life. And something for us to remember too."

Elizabeth Taylor, in Father of the Bride

Throughout history and across cultures, the celebration of a marriage has never failed to generate intense discussion over what to wear. Still today the bride-to-be and her entourage of friends and female family members typically spend many months contemplating and planning their outfits. For, unlike other types of parties, the wedding celebration is a curious mix of fashion and fastidious adherence to custom.

Guests are expected to make an effort to show their appreciation of the bride and mark the enormity of the occasion. Yet it is considered in the worst possible taste for any female guest to draw attention from the

bride by looking excessively "done" — too sexy, too blousy or too conspicuous.

For contemporary advice *Debrett's Etiquette and Modern Manners* offers the following guidelines: "A formal wedding invitation indicates that the dress worn by all guests is expected to be formal too. A wedding provides a good excuse to dress up. Some people enjoy wearing elaborate or formal clothes but others find this too tiresome. The effort involved should be made whenever possible as a compliment to the bride." *Debrett's* also notes that "Hats are invariably worn at weddings together with jewellery, gloves and other smart accessories," and that "Dresses and hats

According to English tradition, the bride and her bridesmaids would walk to the church together. A girl would lead the way, sprinkling petals in the bride's path to wish her a life of happiness. In modern weddings the role of the flower girl is usually restricted to leading the procession once inside the church.

for summer weddings are often more elaborate than at other times of the year as the season lends itself to soft, light materials and exotic colours."

Despite the thousands of words written over the years on wedding dos and dont's, dressing for the day, whether bride or guest, can still be fraught. Dress codes in general are much less rigid than in the past — even black is considered acceptable for a wedding guest to wear these days providing it is in an appropriate style and fabric — but this is only a relatively recent phenomenon. Of course the bride is under intense scrutiny on the day, but so too are the other members of the bridal party, and even guests are not exempt from critique.

The elegant English aristocrat Nancy Mitford was once compelled to write after attending a society wedding that it was "quite splendid & I greatly enjoyed it but oh the get ups I never saw worse. I'm sure English women are dowdier than when I was young. The hats were nearly all as though made by somebody who had once heard about flowers but never seen one — huge muffs of horror." Again, writing in *Love in a Cold Climate* Nancy Mitford relates the outfit worn by one wedding guest, as recounted by the shrewd Lady Montdore: "How extraordinary Lady Kroesing looked, poor woman. I suppose somebody must have told her that the bridegroom's mother should have a bit of everything in her hat — for luck perhaps. Fur, feathers and a scrap of lace — it was all there and a diamond brooch on top to finish it off nicely. Rose diamonds — I had a good look. It's a funny thing that these people who are supposed to be so rich never seem to have a decent jewel to put on."

For centuries wedding etiquette has been a source of debate and strident opinion, eliciting comment from sources as diverse as Emily Post and E.M. Forster. On the matter of the going away dress, for example, Mrs Post insisted that the woman "should not dress as though about to join a circus parade or the ornaments on a Christmas tree, unless she wants to be stared at and commented on in a way that no one of good breeding can endure." The fact that she was compelled to write such advice indicates that it was a common enough sartorial error amongst brides. The wry E.M Forster was equally opinionated when, at a wedding party, he was asked if he would like to be presented to Queen Mary, sitting opposite in rather elaborate dress. "Good Lord," the author quipped, "I thought it was the wedding cake."

It is not surprising that the wedding party generates such intense feeling. At its most base the marriage is a political alliance, a coming together of two tribes, that of the bride and the groom, and it is rare that there is not at least some niggle on either side as to

Roses are the traditional bouquet for the bride and her party. One style of arranging them is the arm sheaf or so-called "Bernhard" bouquet, inspired by the flowers presented to the actress Sarah Bernhard at the end of each performance.

Everyone loves a royal wedding. They are among the milestone events recorded by the press and never fail to capture the public attention for their scale, pomp and ceremony. Before the spectacle of Charles and Diana's wedding in the spotlight of the television cameras, royal marriages may have been more relaxed. At the wedding of Princess Margaret in 1960 (below), the bridesmaids, including Princess Anne with basket, ran ahead of the bridal party. Ten years earlier Princess Margaret was bridesmaid at the wedding of her cousin, Margaret Elphinstone to Denys Rhodes (opposite).

the suitability of the partner chosen, or the character of some family member or friend of bride or groom. Thus all members of the party feel under pressure to look their best on the momentous occasion.

No wonder that in centuries past, and still today for certain royal or celebrity weddings, crowds gather outside the venue to get a closer look at what everyone is wearing. Some of the most celebrated weddings in history have been hugely significant events, changing the course of history in some cases.

The earliest surviving account of a wedding party is that of the nuptial banquet of Caranus of Macedonia held in the third century BC. He invited only his closest comrades and allies, one of which was the Greek writer Hippolochus who afterwards wrote a detailed account of the party. Unfortunately for students of fashion history, he makes no mention of the bride or what she wore, but his description of the event does show the magnitude of the party and its political significance, for the groom took the opportunity to ingratiate himself with his influential guests by showering them with expensive gifts.

Just twenty guests were invited, and at each of the many dinner courses the food and drink was served in platters, plates, bowls and goblets of pure gold and silver, bronze and ivory. As they finished eating and drinking each course the lucky attendees passed the

For her wedding in Switzerland to Mel Ferrer in September 1954 Audrey Hepburn wore a demure dress with high collar by Hubert de Givenchy. In the Elizabethan tradition, the bride wears a wreath of flowers in her hair instead of carrying a bouquet.

precious plates and vessels to their servants standing behind, ready to receive the next treasure.

Hippolochus writes of "a silver platter with a golden edge of no inconsiderable depth, of such a size as to receive the entire bulk of a roast boar of huge size, which lay on its back, showing his belly uppermost, stuffed with many good things" and of a platter of silver placed before each guest on which lay "geese and hares and kids and other rolls curiously made and doves and turtledoves and partridges, and every other kind of bird imaginable in the greatest abundance." All this was washed down with the finest quality wines of the ancient world. "And while we were now all amusing ourselves with agreeable trifling," continues the Greek writer, "some flute-playing women and musicians, and some Rhodian players on the sambuca came in … and others came in succession, each of them bearing two bottles of perfume, bound with a golden thong, and one of the cruets was silver and the other gold, each holding a cotyla [about a pint or 500ml], and they presented them to each of the guests."

The high standard set by Caranus was the inspiration for another grand wedding party that took place several hundred years later, at the marriage of Maria de Medici in Florence in 1600. The account of Caranus' wedding banquet had been published in scholarly texts and would have been reasonably well known to those in the habit of throwing great feasts. In any case, the Florentines were determined to make Maria de Medici's nuptial celebrations unforgettable. It is understandable that the royal court in Florence was so determined to mark the occasion in lavish

The fairytale wedding is usually the preserve of princesses, but these days many woman aspire to the romance of the grand Victorian-style wedding gown, this one by Lisa Gowing (right). For her 1956 wedding to Prince Rainier, Grace Kelly wore a dress by MGM costume designer Helen Rose (overleaf), part of an agreement the actress made with the film studio in return for release her from her contract.

style. The marriage was a power match of impressive scale. The wedding and subsequent days of revelry would mark not only Maria's marriage to King Henry IV, but, more significantly for her family, her transformation into Queen of France. There was only one thing that marred the special day — the groom could not attend. This was not as shocking as it seems by modern standards. If a reigning monarch declined to leave his or her own sovereignty it was not unusual for the marriage to take place by proxy. It would then typically be celebrated again when the bride, or groom, arrived at their new home.

After much delay, the wedding date was finally set for the 5th of October. "On the eve of the wedding," writes Carolin C. Young in *Apples of Gold in Settings of Silver*, "the anticipation reached a feverish pitch as crowds lined the streets to watch the arrival of Cardinal Pietro Aldobrandini." He was met by the Grand Duke of Tuscany (Maria's uncle) at the city gates and escorted through the streets by a huge entourage which included "Florence's handsomest noble pages wearing white with gold sashes, pearl collars and velvet caps" and more than five hundred citizens and foreign guests dressed in "shimmering silks and velvets of red, purple, gold and black," colours reserved for the upper echelons of society. The next day, an even greater crowd assembled to witness the wedding procession to the cathedral, led by high-standing citizens of Florence, followed by 120 of the Grand Duke's men in gold livery, distinguished foreign guests who walked behind the bride's carriage, and the city's most elegant ladies walking hand in hand. Bringing up the rear were 247 young virgins dressed in white with silver trim.

Unlike other festivities, the wedding party calls for a distinct dress code for bride and guests. While guests must make a special effort to be well attired they are never to outshine the bride. Wedding gown by Carlo Pignatelli.

The procession would have made a dazzling sight, but once at the cathedral, all eyes were on the bride, who emerged from her red carriage wearing a white dress, thickly embroidered with gold and encrusted with some of the most dazzling jewels from her enormous dowry, said to be enough to wipe out half of the national debt of France.

Historically the clothing worn at a wedding party was the finest possible. Marriage, particularly among royalty and other wealthy members of society, signalled a political alliance intended to increase the power of both parties involved. Thus it was critical that the bride was attired in the most splendid costume — the costly fabrics and jewels she wore attested to the status and position of her family. Guests likewise took the opportunity to show off their social standing, as distinct from their fashionability or elegance.

Maria's extravagant dress was just a taste of things to come at the banquet, which took place in the vast Salone dei Cinquecento of the Palazzo Vecchio. A team of top designers and artists had been rallied to decorate the splendid hall. Carolin C. Young describes how "the centre of the room was dominated by two fantastic grottoes, sprouting an abundance of trees and foliage." Alongside stood silvered statuary and six gilded statues of the virtues, while at the southern end of the room a huge credenza made of semi-precious stones and marble displayed a selection of

the rarest pieces in the Duke's collection, including exquisite Chinese porcelain and superb pieces from the newly established Venetian glassworks.

"The focal point of the entire scheme was the Queen's Table," explains Carolin C. Young. "The table's crisp white linen cloth from Rheims provided a snowy background for a miniature replica of a winter hunt scene, which densely covered its surface. Confectionary trees and shrubbery, bulls, horses, rabbits, deer, and even a rhinoceros and an elephant, scurried from hunters. The sides of the table had been studded with jewels." In addition were "sugar sculptures in the Hercules theme." The author explains that "Although Christopher Columbus had expanded the sugar supply by introducing cane plants to the Caribbean in 1493, it was still a precious commodity, stored in locked silver boxes, and for courtly banquets, an artistic medium that warranted handling by the most gifted talents." Many of the masterpieces created in sugar for Maria's wedding feast by Pietro Taca, such as Nessus and Deianira, were later cast in bronze and found their way into the collections of museums such as the Louvre, the Frick and the Hermitage.

Aside from the decoration, the array of food at the wedding banquet was astonishing. The royal meal began with a selection of thirty cold dishes, which comprised, among other delicacies, of fig-stuffed

⟶ The long lean line of this dress by Carlo Pignatelli recalls the bias-cut, figure-hugging style of Mainbocher's wedding ensemble for Wallis Simpson for her marriage to the Prince of Wales in 1936.

jellies, peacocks in their plumage, pastry fortresses stuffed with game birds, tarts in the shapes of cranes, boars, dragons and unicorns. Next came the first hot course of eighteen dishes, including roasted game birds, spicy veal breasts and rabbit *alla francese*, followed by a further course of roasts and pies. Then issued truffle tartlets, fritters, cakes and pastries, jellied quinces, fresh and candied fruits as well as olives, fish in wine, eggs and artichokes. Interspersed between courses were entertainments ranging from dexterous displays by Italy's master carvers, who could spear whole roasts and hold them aloft while carving so that delicate slices fell precisely on to the plates of diners, to majestic singing by Vittoria Archilei, the most famous Roman singer of the day.

Although the spectacle of Maria de Medici's banquet seems astonishing and excessive by modern standards, the underlying motivations and emotions remain surprisingly unchanged. As Carolin C. Young points out, "The pressure of a wedding banquet for two newly linked families to overlook differences in taste and tradition exceeds that of a casual evening among friends. The bride, more than anyone else present, bears the stress of unifying the divergent personalities brought together in her honour."

One can well imagine, then, the panic of Princess Elisabeth, eldest daughter of King James I, when her marriage to Prince Frederick was announced with less then six weeks to prepare. Even the most unflappable of modern brides would have trouble finding the right dress for herself and her bridesmaids in that space of time. In this case, the royal couple were betrothed on December 27, 1612, with the wedding date set for Sunday, February 14. The happy event was marred by the death of the bride's beloved older brother several weeks before the betrothal. Thus at her engagement party Elisabeth wore a gown of black satin, brocaded with silver, and a plume of white feathers in her hair,

Christian Lacroix has said that "a wedding dress is one woman's dream of being centre stage, as though it were theatre or ballet." Fittingly, the finale of most couture shows features a bride. Nina Ricci's 1950s bridal gown (below) almost resembles a costume in its scale and detail. Mariana Hardwick's dress (opposite) is also worthy of a diva.

❦ ∽ The white wedding dress has its origins in the sixteenth century, when Mary Queen of Scots wore white for her wedding at Notre Dame to Francis, son of King Henri II of France. The French considered this to be controversial because white was their colour of mourning.

symbolising both her mourning for her brother and her joy at her forthcoming wedding. Despite the rushed preparations Elisabeth did have the whole of the English court at her disposal to help. The royal tailors worked around the clock to complete an enormous trousseau for the bride as well as costumes for her bridesmaids and for the performers in the court masque.

When the day of the wedding arrived the bridal party and guests descended on the chapel of Whitehall Palace for the ceremony. The chapel was small and the guest list had to be strictly curtailed to prevent overcrowding. The fashionable wide caged skirts, called farthingales, had been banned for the wedding festivities (to allow more space for guests) but even this did not stop the Princess ordering six farthingales of taffeta and six of damask for her trousseau.

The young bride must have looked exceptional in her richly embroidered dress made in cloth of silver, with a tight-fitting bodice to the waist and sleeves embroidered with diamonds, then the rich fabric cascading over a wide-spreading farthingale. Her long train was carried by at least a dozen attendants. She wore a gold crown embedded with pearls and diamonds and the long braids of her hair were interwoven with rolls of gold spangles and precious stones. Prince Frederick looked equally dashing in cloth of silver embellished with gold and diamonds. The King wore black velvet and chose his largest and most precious diamond to wear in his hat. The mother of the bride, Queen Anne, dressed for the occasion in a high ruff and a dress of white satin embellished with jewels.

According to costume historian James Laver, "The subjects had vied with the royal party in wearing the most magnificent dress, and the Venetian ambassador reported that the massed effect was beyond imagination. The King afterwards estimated that the value of his jewels, with those of the Queen and Prince Charles, was £90,000." No one wanted to miss out on the excitement. As James Laver explains, "Even poor Arabella Stuart, long imprisoned in the Tower and never to be released, bought herself four new gowns, one of which cost £1,500, to celebrate the occasion." Several days of feasting and court entertainment marked the royal wedding, the first to have taken place on English soil for sixty years. Unfortunately for the King, the expense of it had run to more than £50,000 and the Exchequer was bankrupted. The happy event was quickly curtailed and an additional tax was raised to try and compensate. Presumably King James is not the only father of the bride to have felt the pinch from a daughter's lavish nuptials.

In the case of Marie Antoinette it was the bride's mother who spent vast sums on her daughter's trousseau, in order to make her a fitting bride for the French king-to-be. The Empress of Austria and Queen of Hungary, Maria-Theresa spent four hundred thousand livres on French-made gowns and accessories (about a hundred times as much as

Despite the acceptance of white as the "traditional" colour for the bride, wedding dresses in other colours were common prior to the nineteenth century. Although red, green, brown and black were generally not considered auspicious or appropriate, brides did wear blue, grey and yellow. Pink was also popular, especially for a May wedding. Dress with white bodice and pink skirt by Lorenzo Riva.

a wealthy aristocratic couple would have spent on their combined wardrobes). She can surely not have anticipated that during her daughter's journey in May 1770 to meet her betrothed at Versailles, all the finery she had brought with her from Austria would be confiscated, symbolising the start of her new life in France.

Heartbreakingly for the bride, on her arrival at Versailles she found that the wedding dress that had been chosen for her, although very beautiful, was too small. Caroline Weber explains in *Queen of Fashion* that "the silver gown was enhanced by masses of exquisite white diamonds, which she had received as wedding gifts from her mother, and which accentuated her official standing as the most important woman at court. The ensemble would have been a masterpiece but for one tiny detail … the dressmakers who had confected the wedding gown had misestimated her measurements, and cut the bodice far too small. Try as they might, Marie Antoinette's helpers could not close the dress in back; there remained, as one of the wedding guests observed 'quite a broad strip of lacing and shift quite visible, which had a bad effect between two broader stripes of diamonds.'"

The wedding was taking place that same day so there was no time to make adjustments. She would have to appear before the critical gaze of the entire court of Versailles in a wedding dress that gaped rather badly at the back. As Caroline Weber concludes, "This was a not insignificant glitch, for the bride was supposed to embody the splendour of the dynasty she was joining." It is perhaps little wonder that Marie Antoinette later went to such pains to perfect her appearance during her reign as Queen.

The dress worn by Marie Antoinette adhered to the protocol for a royal wedding, which stipulated that royal brides should wear a gown made from cloth of silver. It followed the fashionable lines of the day, but in itself was quite separate from fashion. In that regard, it is not so different from the dresses that have been worn by brides ever since. Despite its quite unique status in the world of dress, few items of clothing have generated as much critique or detailed description over the centuries, particularly in the days before mass photographic reproduction in magazines and newspapers.

In the influential French style magazine of the late nineteenth century, *La Dernière Mode*, for example, the fashion editor Marguerite de Ponty goes to great pains to describe wedding dresses that she considered to be ideal for the bride of the day. "I have just seen a delightful vision at La Trinité Church," she writes in the fourth edition of 1874, "which prompts me to add, after a quick impression of its lace and flowers, some notes on contemporary etiquette relating to our presence at the ceremony. A wedding dress is

Royal brides of the Renaissance wore gowns made from cloth of silver, richly decked with precious jewels, often part of their dowry. Collette Dinnigan's elegant tiered column references both. For her marriage in 1613 Princess Elizabeth I, eldest daughter of King James I of England, wore a gown of cloth of silver, with diamond-encrusted sleeves. Afterwards, for the wedding ball, she changed into a dress made from cloth of gold, in keeping with her new status as a married woman.

Many brides opt for a naturalistic look, with dresses that gently contour the body, combined with simple hair and flowers. These designs by Grimaldi Giardina (below) and Amanda Wakeley (opposite) could easily be worn at a formal occasion without looking out of place.

Dress codes have relaxed considerably for weddings and brides now feel free to choose from the fashionable looks of any given year, rather than sticking to a particular historical wedding style. Dresses here by Amanda Wakeley (opposite) and Toni Maticevski (below).

≈ *Photographed for the press after their marriage at Rhode Island in 1953, Senator John Kennedy and his bride Jacqueline (née Bouvier) sit down together to begin eating a pineapple salad at their outdoor wedding reception (above and opposite). Jacqueline wore an ivory silk taffeta dress, designed by Ann Lowe, and a rosepoint lace veil that had belonged to her grandmother. Her bridesmaids wore pink faille silk gowns and matching Tudor caps.*

not meant to impress. One simply accepts it as it is: mysterious; following fashion and not following fashion; tempering contemporary taste with vague reminiscences of the distant past; and hiding brand new details under the conventional, as with a veil.

"The costume was as follows: a white satin underskirt covered with a tarlatan skirt, each flounce finishing with a ruche; there were at least twenty on the train, but I only counted four on the front. Tunic pleated crosswise and attached to the skirt; on the bottom of the tunic, a fringe decorated with white pearl. A broad satin sash to one side, falling on to the tunic and attached to the train with a bow: this with a bow was itself attached to the skirt with a crown of orange blossom with a train. The bodice was high and had basques, completely lined with satin, as were the sleeves; and all the trimming of the basques consisted of an ample chicorée [a ruche in the shape of a chicory leaf] and a bouquet of orange blossom, placed to one side, towards the shoulder. A veil of tulle illusion and orange blossom skilfully intertwined in the hair. Everything at once worldly and virginal, and giving no hint of a ball gown, which

would have been a grave fault of taste. No, somehow rich and yet light and suggestive of reserve."

The columnist responded on another occasion to a reader's request for advice on what to wear to her upcoming wedding. Madame de Ponty suggested the following: "Wedding dress in white satin, with smooth crêpe flounces with sharp pleats; cachepoint [ornamental work to conceal stitching] in white jet; a tunic scarf in white satin, trimmed with a flounce like those on the skirt. (With a bow on the train and one of the flaps held back at the waist, this tunic will be enchanting.) A train of orange blossoms going from the waistband and finishing in the bow of the train proper. The bodice has rounded basques, very long in front and very short at the back. A ruff of smooth gauze edged with a garland of orange blossom."

The writer was at pains to point out that although the style she described was at odds with other fashion advice in the magazine, this was in fact intentional. "When you read here certain details a little different from what our Fashion column defined as the coming style," she writes, "do not think I have described anything unfashionable. Wedding dresses, as an earlier column of ours said, are the last to change; they cling to the established mode. There would be something not quite proper … in a bride's wishing to be in advance of fashion."

Wedding guests were considered to have more freedom in style of dress. Even so, clear guidelines applied. As Madame de Ponty comments: "As for the women guests at this ceremony, Fashion retains its full 'kingship of a day' over them, though subject to

customs which alter over the years … The rule for weddings is double, like Paris herself, divided by her river. Left Bank: no deviation from the traditional

❧ The bride will typically wear white (previous page, right) or ivory, but guests are expected to wear anything other than white. Choices for the wedding guest might include vivid silk shantung (previous page, left), or patterned chiffon (opposite and below).

ceremonial. The costume is special: white hat, and light-coloured dresses with a train, set off by a lace cape. Right Bank (by contrast): the visiting-dress in fashion at the moment. This is the rule, though it applies to both in one particular: the wonderful earrings worn during the day give way (and will continue to) to diamond studs."

Although the changing fashions of everyday clothing have had very little influence on wedding dress styles, the choice of ensemble by influential women has sometimes had an overwhelming impact on what women choose to wear on their wedding day. And inevitably it seems that royal brides have had the most sway in affecting bridal fashions.

Up until the wedding of Queen Victoria, bridal dresses for princesses and queens were of heavily textured brocades, cloth of gold or of silver, and encrusted with jewels. Commoners wore gowns that reflected the prevailing silhouettes and colours of formal dress styles. If white, they tended to be cream or ivory shades, which were considered more flattering to the complexion. But in 1840, when Queen Victoria walked down the aisle to wed Albert of Saxe-Coburg, a new trend in bridal fashion took off. Victoria chose a simple white satin gown, a veil of lace, and a wreath of orange blossom, in place of the ostentatious gowns and golden crowns of her predecessors. The wedding photo was published far

and wide, and suddenly every bride wanted to wear white, and have orange blossoms for her hair.

The trend for white wedding dresses has remained more or less unchallenged ever since, although there have been fashionable deviations. Wallis Simpson chose for her marriage to the Prince of Wales in 1937 a simple, floor-length silk crepe dress with matching jacket in periwinkle blue. On the eve of the wedding *Life* magazine declared that "Women of the world were little absorbed in the conventional satin gowns of England's new Queen. What Mrs Wallis Warfield Simpson would wear, however, roused their avid curiosity." It was not long before copies of the dress were selling in department stores for a fraction of the price of the real thing.

However, almost twenty years later, the wedding of another style icon, this time a Hollywood princess, set the standard for the elegant bride. The year 1956 marks what many at the time considered the wedding of the century, that of Grace Kelly to Prince Rainier of Monaco. Although the couple had wed in private in a civil ceremony on April 18, they held a formal, public wedding the following day in a Catholic Mass at the cathedral in Monaco. The entire event was filmed, much to the couple's distaste, but in order to get out of her contract with MGM Grace Kelly had agreed. Appropriately enough, her gown for the public event was created by MGM costume designer

Where in the 1950s the fashion role models had been Hollywood beauties, from the mid-1960s onwards rock stars and models were the new style icons. At her private wedding to Mick Jagger in St Tropez in 1971, Bianca Perez-Mora Macías opted for a white trouser suit designed by Savile Row tailor Tommy Nutter, and she wore the jacket with nothing but bare skin underneath. In doing so she sparked a vogue for less staid, more fashion-led wedding clothes, like those pictured here.

The wedding guest of the 1970s looked as though she would be equally at home in a smart nightclub. As bridal clothes themselves became more alternative, guests could also relax a little in their choice of attire. Trouser suits, skirt ensembles and jersey dresses, short and long, were all acceptable, and hats were no longer considered essential.

↶⟋⟋⟋⟋ *For many decades, a hat and gloves largely remained unchallenged as the appropriate accessories for wedding guests. Examples here are Yves Saint Laurent's two piece in heavy white linen from 1964 (opposite) with felt hat and long gloves, and a Bill Blass dress with cartwheel hat and leather gloves (above) from 1980.*

Helen Rose and the wardrobe department. The dress was made from antique Valenciennes rose point lace, silk taffeta and tulle. The bride's veil was covered with appliquéd lace lovebirds and seed pearls. Prince Rainier obviously agreed to the filming, designing his own Napoleonic-style dress uniform for the day.

In retrospect, the wedding of the century undoubtedly belongs to Diana, Princess of Wales, whose fairytale wedding was broadcast to a rapt audience of millions. Her romantic, billowing dress of ivory silk ushered in a revival of Victorian dress styles, and countless copies of the "Diana" dress were donned by brides dreaming of a fairytale wedding. Diana's sister-in-law, Sarah Ferguson, followed suit for her marriage to Prince Andrew in a dress with puffed sleeves and crinolined skirt.

Yet several years later, in 1999, at the wedding of the youngest Windsor sibling, Prince Edward, the mood was rather more low-key. The bride, Sophie Rhys-Jones, requested that her guests not wear hats, but several could not quite bear to part with tradition. The Queen Mother at age ninety-eight ignored the request and wore a hat, while several others wore feathers in their hair. And even the bride was not quite able to abandon the high standards demanded of a royal wedding. Her silk-organza and crepe gown, although simple in line, was adorned with 325,000 cut-glass and pearl beads, and boasted a considerable train. Her veil was fixed in place with a diamond tiara borrowed from the Queen. As *Time* magazine reported of the event: "Though they deviated from regal norms in many ways, the couple recited centuries-old vows and consented to a carriage ride through Windsor before returning to the castle for a buffet-dinner reception. In the end, the couple bowed to tradition — but not too deeply."

For the most sensible advice on negotiating the challenges posed by wedding party attire, Emily Post's 1922 book of etiquette still offers sage advice almost a century on: "Everyone knows what a wedding dress is like. It may be of any material, satin, brocade, velvet, chiffon or entirely of lace. It may be embroidered in pearls, crystal or silver; or it may be as plain as a slip-cover — anything in fact that the bride fancies, and made in whatever fashion or period she may choose."

At the royal wedding of Prince Edward to Sophie Rhys-Jones in 1999, the bride requested that guests should not wear hats, a dramatic departure from the norm, yet in keeping with current ideas. Behnaz Sarafpour offers the perfect dress for the contemporary wedding guest — restrained, elegant and polished; no hat required.

Credits

Introduction

Chapter One

Chapter One

Page 44-45
*Courtesy of
Jayson Brundson*

Page 57
*Courtesy of
Gianfranco Ferre*

Page 46
*Roger Viollet/
Getty Images*

Page 58
*The Metropolitan
Museum of Art,
Purchase,
Irene Lewisohn Trust,
1983 (1983.8ab)
Photograph© 1983
The Metropolitan
Museum of Art*

Page 59
*Larry Ellis/
Hulton Archive/
Getty Images*

Page 48
*Courtesy of
Grimaldi Giardina*

Page 49
*Courtesy of
Grimaldi Giardina*

Page 60
*Courtesy of
Blumarine*

Page 61
*Courtesy of
Grimaldi
Giardina*

Page 50
*Courtesy of Chanel
Photograph by Karl
Lagerfeld*

Page 53
*Slim Aarons/
Hulton Archive/
Getty Images*

Page 54
*Harry Benson/
Hulton Archive/
Getty Images*

Chapter Two

Page 82
*Courtesy of
Robinson Valentine*

Page 83
*Courtesy of
Luca Luca*

Page 96
*Courtesy of Bill
Blass Archives*

Page 97
*Bill Eppridge/
Time & Life
Pictures/
Getty Images*

Page 84
*Courtesy of Cecil
Beaton Studio
Archive, Sotheby's*

Page 87
*© SIPA/
Snappermedia*

Page 99
*Courtesy of Cecil
Beaton Studio
Archive, Sotheby's*

Page 88
*Courtesy of Cecil
Beaton Studio
Archive, Sotheby's*

Page 91
*Gordon Parks/
Time & Life
Pictures/
Getty Images*

Page 100
*Courtesy of
Gianfranco Ferre*

Page 101
*Courtesy of
Gianfranco Ferre*

Page 92
*© SIPA/
Snappermedia*

Page 93
*© Album Online/
Snappermedia*

Page 102
*Courtesy of Luca Luca
Photograph by Michael
Thompson*

Page 103
*Courtesy of
Luca Luca*

Page 94
*© SIPA/
Snappermedia*

Page 104
*Courtesy of
Martin Grant*

Page 105
*Courtesy of
Lisa Ho*

Chapter Two

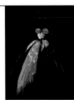

Chapter Three

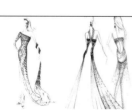

Chapter Three

Page 173
Courtesy of
Alice McCall

Page 183
Courtesy of
Chanel
Photograph by
Karl Lagerfeld

Page 174
Courtesy of
Reem Acra

Page 175
Courtesy of
Martin Grant

Page 184
Courtesy of
Gianfranco Ferre

Page 185
Courtesy of
Bill Blass Archives

Page 176
Courtesy of
Bill Blass Archives

Page 177
Courtesy of
Givenchy

Page 186
Courtesy of BluGirl
Photograph by
Michelangelo Di
Battista

Page 188
Courtesy of
Emilio Pucci

Page 178
Courtesy of
Tina Kalivas
Photograph by
Georges Antoni

Page 179
Courtesy of
Tina Kalivas
Photograph by
Georges Antoni

Page 190
Courtesy of
Emilio Pucci

Page 191
Courtesy of
Emilio Pucci

Page 180
Courtesy of
Carla Zampatti

Page 181
Courtesy of
Escada

Page 192
Courtesy of
Gianfranco Ferre

Chapter Three

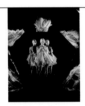

Page 218
Courtesy of
Blumarine
Photograph by
Craig McDean

Page 228
Courtesy of
Carla Zampatti

Page 229
Courtesy of
Carla Zampatti

Page 220
Courtesy of
Chanel
Photograph by
Karl Lagerfeld

Page 221
Courtesy of
Chaiken

Page 230
Courtesy of
Tina Kalivas
Photograph by
Georges Antoni

Page 231
Courtesy of
Collette Dinnigan
Photograph by
Robert Erdmann

Page 223
Courtesy of
Filippa K
Photograph by
Patrik Sehlstedt
Agency: Adamsky

Page 225
Courtesy of
Chanel
Photograph by
Karl Lagerfeld

Page 226-227
Courtesy of
La Perla
Photograph by
Vincent Peters
Model: Bianca Balti

Chapter Four

Page 257
Courtesy of
Collette Dinnigan
Photograph by
Robert Erdmann

Page 267
Courtesy of
Lisa Ho

Page 258
Courtesy of
Etro
Photograph by
Stefane Sedanoui

Page 268
Courtesy of
Derek Lam

Page 260
Courtesy of
Carven

Page 261
Courtesy of
Luca Luca

Page 262
Courtesy of
Lisa Ho

Page 264-265
Courtesy of
Lisa Ho

Chapter Five

Page 292
*Courtesy of
Lorenzo Riva*

Page 294
*Courtesy of
Collette Dinnigan*

Page 304
*Courtesy of
J Mendel*

Page 305
*Courtesy of Peter
Som*

Page 296
*Courtesy of Grimaldi
Giardina*

Page 297
*Courtesy of
Amanda Wakeley*

Page 306
*Courtesy of Bill
Blass archives*

Page 298
*Courtesy of
Amanda Wakeley*

Page 299
*Courtesy of Toni
Maticevski*

Page 308
*Courtesy of Bill
Blass Archives*

Page 300
*Lisa Larsen/
Time & Life
Pictures/
Getty Images*

Page 301
*Lisa Larsen/
Time & Life
Pictures/
Getty Images*

Page 310
*Courtesy of Bill
Blass Archives*

Page 311
*Barry Lategan/
Hulton Archive/
Getty Images*

Page 302
*Courtesy of à la
disposition.*

Page 303
*Courtesy of à la
disposition.*

Page 312
*Courtesy of
Behnaz Sarafpour*

Additional
credits:
Page 316 *Dress by
Badgley Mischka
Photograph by
Joshua Allen*

Page 332
*Courtesy of Chanel
Photograph by
Karl Lagerfeld*

Selected Bibliography

Aretz, Gertrude. *The Elegant Woman: From the Rococo Period to Modern Times*. Harcourt, Brace & Company, New York, 1932

Beard, Patricia. *After the Ball: Gilded Age Secrets and the Party that Ignited the Great Wall Street Scandal of 1905*. Harper Collins Publishers, New York, 2003

Beaton, Cecil. *The Glass of Fashion*. Weidenfeld and Nicholson, London, 1954

Blume, Mary. *Côte d'Azur: Inventing the French Riviera*. Thames and Hudson, London, 1994

Bluttal, Steven, ed.; Mears, Patricia. *Halston*. Phaidon Press, London, 2001

Dariaux, Genevieve Antoine. *A Guide to Elegance: For Every Woman Who Wants to Be Well and Properly Dressed on all Occasions*. Harper Collins Publishers, London, 2003

Davis, Deborah. *Party of the Century; The Fabulous Story of Truman Capote and His Black and White Ball*. John Wiley & Sons, New Jersey, 2006

Dwight, Eleanor. *Diana Vreeland*. William Morrow, New York, 2002

Etherington-Smith, Meredith and Pilcher, Jeremy. *The 'It' Girls: Elinor Glyn, Novelist and her sister Lucile, Couturiere*. Harcourt Brace Jovanovich Publishers, Orlando, 1986

Evans, Caroline. 'Masks, Mirrors and Mannequins: Elsa Schiaparelli and the Decentred Subject'. In *Fashion Theory*, Volume 3, Issue 1, March 1999, Berg

Fogarty, Anne. *Wife-Dressing: The Fine Art of Being a Well–Dressed Wife*. Julian Messner, New York, 1959

Goetz, Adrian. *Marie-Antoinette Style*. Assouline, New York, 2005

Gregory, Alexis. *Families of Fortune: Life in the Gilded Age*. Rizzoli International Publications, New York, 1993

Hergesheimer, Joseph. *The Party Dress*. Grosset & Dunlap, New York, 1930

Kladstrup, Don and Kladstrup, Petie. *Champagne: How the World's Most Glamorous Wine Triumphed Over War and Hard Times*. William Morrow, New York, 2005

Laver, James. *Costume & Fashion: A Concise History*. Thames and Hudson, London, 1969 and 1982

Laver, James. *Memorable Balls*. Derek Verschoyle, London, 1954

Lehnert, Gertrud. *A History of Fashion in the 20th Century*. Könemann, Cologne, 2000

MacCarthy, Fiona. *Last Curtsey: The End of the Debutantes*. Faber and Faber, London 2006

McDowell, Colin, ed. *The Pimlico Companion to Fashion*. Pimlico, London, 1998

Mansfield, Katherine. *The Garden Party and Other Stories*. Penguin Books, London, 2000

Martin, Richard. *Versace*. Thames and Hudson, London, 1997

Maxwell, Elsa. *R.S.V.P.: Elsa Maxwell's Own Story*. Little Brown, New York, 1954

Morgan, John. *Debrett's New Guide to Etiquette and Modern Manners*. Headline, London, 1999

Mulvagh, Jane. *Vogue: History of 20th Century Fashion*. Bloomsbury Books, 1992

Murphy, Sophia. *The Duchess of Devonshire's Ball*. Sidgwick & Jackson, London, 1984

Porter, Cecil. *Not Without a Chaperone: Modes and Manners from 1897 to 1914*. New English Library, London, 1972

Nicholson, Juliet. *The Perfect Summer: Dancing into Shadow; England in 1911*. John Murray, London, 2006

Pochna, Marie-France. *Christian Dior: The Man Who Made the World Look New*. Arcade Publishing, New York, 1996

Post, Emily. *Etiquette*. Funk & Wagnalls, New York, 1922

Purbank, P.N.; Cain, A.M. *Mallarmé on Fashion: A Translation of the Fashion Magazine 'La Dernière Mode', with Commentary*. Berg, London 2004

Ryersson, Scott D. and Yaccarino, Michael Orlando. *Infinite Variety: The Life and Legend of the Marchesa Casati*. Pimlico, London, 2000

Steele, Valerie. *Fifty Years of Fashion: New Look to Now*. Yale University Press, New Haven and London, 2000

Stuart, Amanda Mackenzie. *Consuelo and Alva Vanderbilt: The Story of a Daughter and a Mother in the Gilded Age*. Harper Collins Publishers, New York, 2005

Vreeland, Diana. *DV*. Da Capo Press, New York, 1984

Weber, Caroline. *Queen of Fashion: What Marie Antoinette Wore to the Revolution*. Aurum Press, London, 2006

Young, Carolin, C. *Apples of Gold in Settings of Silver: Stories of Dinner as a Work of Art*. Simon & Schuster, New York, 2002

Zeitz, Joshua. *Flapper: A Madcap Story of Sex, Style, Celebrity and the Women Who Made America*. Three Rivers Press, New York, 2006

Coco Chanel maintained that "a girl should be two things: classy and fabulous." Black fringed cocktail dress by Karl Lagerfeld for Chanel.

Index

Acknowledgements

The author would like to thank the following people for their much-valued personal support: Bradd and Daisy Nicholls, Melissa Kelly, Rachel Robinson, Freya Salter.

And, for their professional assistance and creative contribution:
Susie Stenmark and colleagues at Chanel, Sally Pitt at Giorgio Armani, Lynda and Daniel Kinne at à la disposition, Lisa Gowing, Ian Barry, Rebekah Malone at Mariana Hardwick, Alice McCall, Mat Pal, Lisa Anne, Danielle Cusack Scott, the team at Snapper Media, Gabriella Alessi at Carla Zampatti, Caroline Eriksson at Filippa K and Lisa Dempsey at Jac and Jack Liza Seville and Georgina Turner at Getty Images, Joanna Ling, Katherine Marshall and Sue Daly at Sotheby's, Gabriel Scarvelli, Jayson Brundson, Felicity Van Rysbergen and Trish at Line Communications, Toni Maticevski, Lisa Ho, Rachael Myers at Bill Blass Archives, Frank Pulice at Carmen Marc Valvo, Joshua Allen, Reem Acra, Nancy at Atelier PR, Arthur Elgort's studio, Richard Chai and Jessica Lasota, Annabelle Dunne at Catherine Malandrino, Stéphanie Gibert at Nina Ricci, Jean Yu, Tara Lefkowitz and Ly at Jean Yu, Valeria Ricci and Victoria Hennessy at Etro, Flaminia d'Onofrio at Blumarine, Paola Giannini and Regina Cacciavillani and at Emilio Pucci, Bridet Bowen at Amanda Wakeley, Maud Michel at Martin Grant, Ana Oliveira at Carolina Herrera, Sophie Trippe-Smith and Seamus Dinnigan at Collette Dinnigan, Minsi Cordingley at Robinson Valentine, Beth Shapiro at Marchesa, Beth Sturm and Zac Posen, Wayne Conway at Kate Sylvester, Camilla Orlandi and Grazia Venneri at Gucci, Giuseppina Graham at Prada, Christian Barraclough, Laura Giudici at La Perla.

Most importantly, sincere thanks to Beatrice Vincenzini and David Shannon at Co & Bear.